CCNP

SWITCH 642-813
Quick Reference

Denise Donohue, CCIE No. 9566

Cisco Press

800 East 96th Street

Indianapolis, Indiana 46240 USA

CCNP SWITCH 642-813 Quick Reference

Denise Donohue

Copyright® 2010 Pearson Education, Inc.

Published by:
Cisco Press
800 East 96th Street
Indianapolis, IN 46240 USA

Printed in the United States of America

Third Printing: March 2012

ISBN-13: 978-1-58720-318-3

ISBN-10: 1-58720-318-9

Publisher
Paul Boger

Associate Publisher
Dave Dusthimer

Executive Editor
Brett Bartow

Project Editor
Jennifer Gallant

Managing Editor
Patrick Kanouse

Editorial Assistant
Vanessa Evans

Designer
Sandra Schroeder

Warning and Disclaimer

Trademark Acknowledgments

Corporate and Government Sales

The publisher offers excellent discounts on this book when ordered in quantity for bulk purchases or special sales, which may include electronic versions and/or custom covers and content particular to your business, training goals, marketing focus, and branding interests. For more information, please contact:

U.S. Corporate and Government Sales   1-800-382-3419

corpsales@pearsontechgroup.com

For sales outside the United States please contact:

International Sales   international@pearsoned.com

Feedback Information

At Cisco Press, our goal is to create in-depth technical books of the highest quality and value. Each book is crafted with care and precision, undergoing rigorous development that involves the unique expertise of members from the professional technical community.

Readers' feedback is a natural continuation of this process. If you have any comments regarding how we could improve the quality of this book, or otherwise alter it to better suit your needs, you can contact us through email at feedback@ciscopress.com. Please make sure to include the book title and ISBN in your message.

We greatly appreciate your assistance.

Americas Headquarters	Asia Pacific Headquarters	Europe Headquarters
Cisco Systems, Inc.	Cisco Systems, Inc.	Cisco Systems International BV
170 West Tasman Drive	168 Robinson Road	Haarlerbergpark
San Jose, CA 95134-1706	#28-01 Capital Tower	Haarlerbergweg 13-19
USA	Singapore 068912	1101 CH Amsterdam
www.cisco.com	www.cisco.com	The Netherlands
Tel: 408 526-4000	Tel: +65 6317 7777	www-europe.cisco.com
800 553-NETS (6387)	Fax: +65 6317 7799	Tel: +31 0 800 020 0791
Fax: 408 527-0883		Fax: +31 0 20 357 1100

Cisco has more than 200 offices worldwide. Addresses, phone numbers, and fax numbers are listed on the Cisco Website at **www.cisco.com/go/offices.**

About the Authors

Denise Donohue, CCIE No. 9566, is a senior solutions architect for ePlus Technology, a Cisco Gold partner. She works as a consulting engineer, designing networks for ePlus' customers. Prior to this role, she was a systems engineer for the data consulting arm of SBC/AT&T. She has co-authored several Cisco Press books in the areas of route/switch and voice. Denise has worked as a Cisco instructor and course director for Global Knowledge and was a network consultant for many years. Her areas of specialization include route/switch, voice, and data center.

About the Technical Editors

'Rhette (Margaret) Marsh has been working in the networking and security industry for over ten years, and has extensive experience with internetwork design, IPv6, forensics, and greyhat work. She currently is a design consultant for Cisco in San Jose, CA, and works primarily with the Department of Defense and contractors. Before this, she worked extensively both in the financial industry as a routing and switching and design/security consultant and also in an attack attribution and forensics context. She currently holds a CCIE in Routing and Switching (CCIE No. 17476), CCNP, CCDP, CCNA, CCDA, CISSP and is working towards her Security and Design CCIEs. In her copious free time, she enjoys number theory, arcane literature, cycling, hiking in the redwoods, sea kayaking, and her mellow cat, lexx.

Contents at a Glance

Contents

Icons Used in This Book

Router   Route/Switch Processor   Multilayer Switch   Workgroup Switch   PC

Command Syntax Conventions

The conventions used to present command syntax in this book are the same conventions used in the IOS Command Reference. The Command Reference describes these conventions as follows:

- **Boldface** indicates commands and keywords that are entered literally as shown. In actual configuration examples and output (not general command syntax), boldface indicates commands that are manually input by the user (such as a **show** command).

- *Italic* indicates arguments for which you supply actual values.

- Vertical bars (|) separate alternative, mutually exclusive elements.

- Square brackets ([ ]) indicate an optional element.

- Braces ({ }) indicate a required choice.

- Braces within brackets ([{ }]) indicate a required choice within an optional element.

Introduction

The Cisco Certified Network Professional (CCNP®) Routing and Switching certification validates knowledge and skills required to install, configure and troubleshoot converged local and wide area networks with 100 to 500 or more nodes. With a CCNP Routing and Switching certification, a network professional demonstrates the knowledge and skills required to manage the routers and switches that form the network core, as well as edge applications that integrate voice, wireless, and security into the network.

The *CCNP SWITCH 642-813 Quick Reference* was written to help you prepare for the *SWITCH 642-813* exam in the CCNP Routing and Switching certification. Some readers tell us that they use this book before beginning their exam preparation, to find which areas they are weak in. This helps target their studying. Others use it after studying or taking the course as a concise learning resource during their final preparation for the exam.

This book will also help once your exams are over, when you need a quick answer about a technology, or a reminder about configuration steps.

Who Should Read This Book?

Current and aspiring network engineers will find this book useful in two ways. First, those preparing for the CCNP Routing and Switching certification will appreciate the targeted review of exam topics. It will help them understand the technologies, not just memorize questions. This will lead to success on the exam and improved on-the-job performance. Secondly, the book serves as a reference for those not pursuing the certification. Its short descriptions and many examples come in handy when you need a fast answer to a question, or to configure something quickly. It deserves a place on every network engineer's bookshelf.

How This Book Is Organized

Following is a description for each section.

Chapter 1: Campus Network Design

Chapter 1 covers design considerations for small, medium, and large campuses, and Data Centers. It describes the Service-Oriented Network Architecture (SONA) and how it applies to campus design. The PPDIOO model is shown as a way to plan network implementations.

Chapter 2: VLAN Implementation

This chapter gives an overview of VLANs, then describes VLAN design and implementation planning. It covers trunking, VTP, and EtherChannel including best practices, configuration, and troubleshooting.

Chapter 3: Spanning Tree

Chapter 3 goes into detail on Spanning-Tree, Rapid Spanning-Tree, and Multiple Spanning Tree. It covers spanning-tree tuning mechanisms such as UDLD, loop guard, backbonefast, and BPDUguard. It also includes troubleshooting Spanning-Tree and Spanning-Tree best practices.

Chapter 4: InterVLAN Routing

Routing between VLANs using a router and using a multilayer switched are both covered in Chapter 4. This chapter additionally describes switch forwarding architectures and goes into detail on CEF operation and configuration.

Chapter 5: Implementing High Availability

This chapter describes the components of high availability - redundancy, technology, people, processes, and tools. It goes into depth on achieving network resiliency through correct network design. It also describes the role that network management tools Syslog, SNMP, and IP SLA play in a highly available network.

Chapter 6: First Hop Redundancy

Chapter 6 looks at HSRP, VRRP, and GLBP. It describes their operation, the differences between them, how to configure them, and how to tune them, It covers best practices planning and implementation.

Chapter 7: Campus Network Security

This chapter is concerned with ways that the LAN might be attacked and its security compromised. It covers four types of attacks: MAC address attacks, VLAN-based attacks, spoofing attacks, and attacks against the switch itself. Prevention techniques are shown for each type of attack.

Chapter 8: Voice and Video in a Campus Network

Chapter 8 describes how to prepare a network for voice over IP and video over IP. It covers the components needed such as a PoE switch, and the QoS requirements of voice and video. The chapter also shows how to configure a switch to support VoIP, including AutoQoS configuration.

Chapter 9: Wireless LANs in a Campus Network

This chapter describes how to integrate wireless into the LAN. It provides an overview of wireless operation and components, and describes how introducing wireless impacts the LAN traffic. The chapter also discusses how to plan a wireless implementation and shows how to configure your switches when connecting to access points or controllers.

SWITCH

CHAPTER 1

Campus Network Design

An enterprise campus generally refers to a network in a specific geographic location. It can be within one building or span multiple buildings near each other. A campus network also includes the Ethernet LAN portions of a network outside the data center. Large enterprises have multiple campuses connected by a WAN. Using models to describe the network architecture divides the campus into several internetworking functional areas, thus simplifying design, implementation, and troubleshooting.

The Hierarchical Design Model

Cisco has used the three-level Hierarchical Design Model for years. The hierarchical design model divides a network into three layers:

- **Access:** Provides end-user access to the network. In the LAN, local devices such as phones and computers access the local network. In the WAN, remote users or sites access the corporate network.

  - High availability via hardware such as redundant power supplies and redundant supervisor engines. Software redundancy via access to redundant default gateways using a first hop redundancy protocol (FHRP).

  - Converged network support by providing access to IP phones, computers, and wireless access points. Provides QoS and multicast support.

  - Security through switching tools such as Dynamic ARP Inspection, DHCP snooping, BPDU Guard, port-security, and IP source guard. Controls network access.

- **Distribution:** Aggregation point for access switches. Provides availability, QoS, fast path recovery, and load balancing.

  - High availability through redundant distribution layer switches providing dual paths to the access switches and to core switches.

Use of FHRP protocols to ensure connectivity if one distribution switch is removed.

- Routing policies applied, such as route selection, filtering, and summarization. Can be default gateway for access devices. QoS and security policies applied.

- Segmentation and isolation of workgroups and workgroup problems from the core, typically using a combination of Layer 2 and Layer 3 switching.

- **Core:** The backbone that provides a high-speed, Layer 3 path between distribution layers and other network segments. Provides reliability and scalability.

  - Reliability through redundant devices, device components, and paths.

  - Scalability through scalable routing protocols. Having a core layer in general aids network scalability by providing gigabit (and faster) connectivity, data and voice integration, and convergence of the LAN, WAN, and MAN.

  - No policies such as ACLs or filters that would slow traffic down.

A set of distribution devices and their accompanying access layer switches are called a switch block.

Core Layer

Is a core layer always needed? Without a core layer, the distribution switches must be fully meshed. This becomes more of a problem as a campus network grows larger. A general rule is to add a core when connecting three or more buildings or four or more pairs of building distribution switches. Some benefits of a campus core are:

- Adds a hierarchy to distribution switch connectivity

- Simplifies cabling because a full-mesh between distribution switches is not required

- Reduces routing complexity by summarizing distribution networks

Small Campus Design

In a small campus, the core and distribution can be combined into one layer. *Small* is defined as fewer than 200 end devices. In very small networks, one multilayer switch might provide the functions of all three layers. Figure 1-1 shows a sample small network with a collapsed core.

Figure 1-1   Small Campus Network

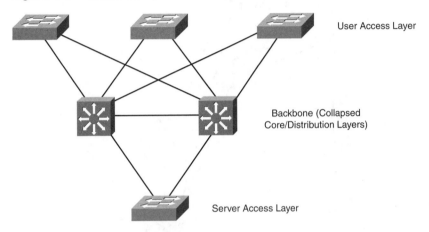

User Access Layer

Backbone (Collapsed Core/Distribution Layers)

Server Access Layer

Medium Campus Design

A medium-sized campus, defined as one with between 200 and 1000 end devices, is more likely to have several distribution switches and thus require a core layer. Each building or floor is a campus block with access switches uplinked to redundant multilayer distribution switches. These are then uplinked to redundant core switches, as shown in Figure 1-2.

Data Center Design

The core layer connects end users to the data center devices. The data center segment of a campus can vary in size from few servers connected to the same switch as users in a small campus, to a separate network with its own three-layer design in a large enterprise. The three layers of a data center model are slightly different:

- **Core layer:** Connects to the campus core. Provides fast switching for traffic into and out of the data center.

- **Aggregation layer:** Provides services such as server load balancing, content switching, SSL off-load, and security through firewalls and IPS.

- **Access layer:** Provides access to the network for servers and storage units. Can be either Layer 2 or Layer 3 switches.

Figure 1-2   Medium-Sized Campus Network

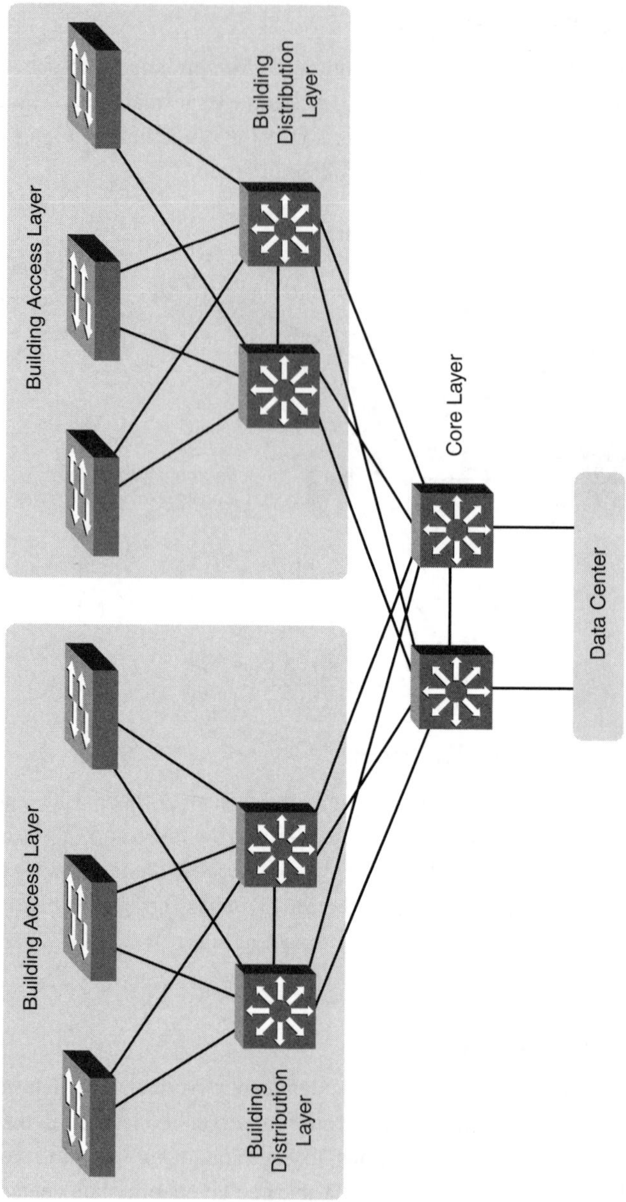

Network Traffic Flow

The need for a core layer and the devices chosen for the core also depend on the type of network traffic and traffic flow patterns. Modern converged networks include different traffic types, each with unique requirements for security, QoS, transmission capacity, and delay. These include

- IP telephony signaling and media

- Core Application traffic, such as Enterprise Resource Programming (ERP), Customer Relationship Management (CRM)

- Multicast multimedia

- Network management

- Application data traffic, such as web pages, email, file transfer, and database transactions

- Scavenger class traffic that requires less-than-best-effort treatment

The different types of applications also have different traffic flow patterns. These might include

- Peer-to-Peer applications such as IP phone calls, video conferencing, file sharing, and instant messaging provides real-time interaction. It might not traverse the core at all, if the users are local to each other. Their network requirements vary, with voice having strict jitter needs and video conferencing using high bandwidth.

- Client-Server applications require access to servers such as email, file storage, and database servers. These servers are typically centralized in a data center, and users require fast, reliable access to them. Server farm access must also be securely controlled to deny unauthorized users.

- Client-Enterprise Edge applications are located on servers at the WAN edge, reachable from outside the company. These can include email and web servers, or e-commerce servers, for example. Access to these servers must be secure and highly available.

Service-Oriented Network Architecture

Service-Oriented Network Architecture (SONA) attempts to provide a design framework for a network that can deliver the services and applications businesses need. It acknowledges that the network connects all components of the business and is critical to them. The SONA model integrates network and application functionality cooperatively and enables the network to be smart about how it handles traffic to minimize the footprint of applications.

Figure 1-3 shows how SONA breaks down this functionality into three layers:

- **Network Infrastructure:** Campus, data center, branch, and so on. Networks and their attached end systems (resources such as servers, clients, and storage.) These can be connected anywhere within the network. The goal is to provide anytime/any place connectivity.

- **Interactive Services:** Resources allocated to applications, using the network infrastructure. These include

  - Management

  - Infrastructure services such as security, mobility, voice, compute, storage, and identity

  - Application delivery

  - Virtualization of services and network infrastructure

- **Applications:** Includes business policy and logic. Leverages the interactive services layer to meet business needs. Has two sublayers:

  - Application layer, which defines business applications

  - Collaboration layer, which defines applications such as unified messaging, conferencing, IP telephony, video, instant messaging, and contact centers

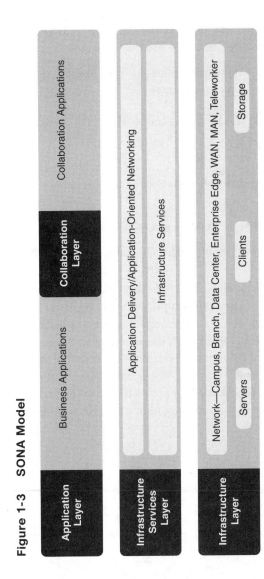

Figure 1-3   SONA Model

Planning a Network Implementation

It is important to use a structured approach to planning and implementing any network changes or new network components. A comprehensive life-cycle approach lowers the total cost of ownership, increases network availability, increases business agility, and provides faster access to applications and services.

The Prepare, Plan, Design, Implement, Operate, and Optimize (PPDIOO) Lifecycle Approach is one structure that can be used. The components are

- **Prepare:** Organizational requirements gathering, high-level architecture, network strategy, business case strategy

- **Plan:** Network requirements gathering, network examination, gap analysis, project plan

- **Design:** Comprehensive, detailed design

- **Implement:** Detailed implementation plan, and implementation following its steps

- **Operate:** Day-to-day network operation and monitoring

- **Optimize:** Proactive network management and fault correction

Network engineers at the CCNP level will likely be involved at the implementation and following phases. They can also participate in the design phase. It is important to create a detailed implementation plan that includes test and verification procedures and a rollback plan. Each step in the implementation plan should include a description, a reference to the design document, detailed implementation and verification instructions, detailed rollback instructions, and the estimated time needed for completion. A complex implementation should be done in sections, with testing at each incremental section.

## CHAPTER 2

VLAN Implementation

VLANs are used to break large campus networks into smaller pieces. The benefit of this is to minimize the amount of broadcast traffic on a logical segment.

VLAN Overview

A virtual LAN (VLAN) is a logical LAN, or a logical subnet. It defines a broadcast domain. A physical subnet is a group of devices that shares the same physical wire. A logical subnet is a group of switch ports assigned to the same VLAN, regardless of their physical location in a switched network. VLAN membership can be assigned either statically by port, or dynamically by MAC address or username.

Two types of VLANs are

- **End-to-end VLAN:** VLAN members reside on different switches throughout the network. They are used when hosts are assigned to VLANs for policy reasons, rather than physical location. This provides users a consistent policy and access to resources regardless of their location. It also makes troubleshooting more complex because so many switches can carry traffic for a specific VLAN, and broadcasts can traverse many switches. Figure 2-1 shows end-to-end VLANs.

- **Local VLAN:** Hosts are assigned to VLANs based on their location, such as a floor in a building. This design is more scalable and easier to troubleshoot because the traffic flow is more deterministic. It enables more redundancy and minimizes failure domains. It does require a routing function to share resources between VLANs. Figure 2-2 shows an example of local VLANs.

When planning a VLAN structure, consider traffic flows and link sizing. Take into account the entire traffic pattern of applications found in your network. For instance, IP voice media traffic travels directly between phones, but signaling traffic must pass to the Unified Communications Manager. Multicast traffic must communicate back to the routing process and possibly call upon a Rendezvous Point. Various user applications, such as email and Citrix, place different demands on the network.

Figure 2-1   End-to-End VLANs

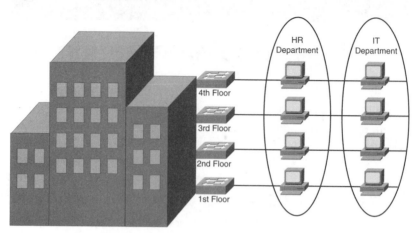

Figure 2-2   Local VLANs

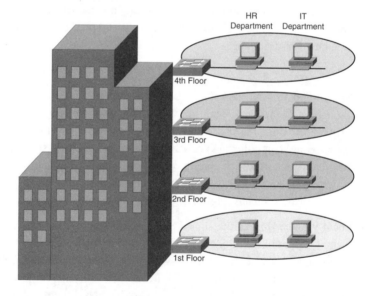

Application flow influences link bandwidth. Remember that uplink ports need to handle all hosts communicating concurrently, and although VLANs logically separate traffic, traffic in different VLANs still travels over the same trunk line. Benchmark throughput for critical application and user data during peak hours; then analyze the results for any bottlenecks throughout the layered design.

User access ports are typically Fast Ethernet or faster. Access switches must have the necessary port density and can be either Layer 2 or Layer 3. Ports from user Access to the Distribution layer should be Gigabit Ethernet or better, with an oversubscription ratio of no more than 20:1. Distribution switches should be multilayer or Layer 3. Links from Distribution to the Core should be Gigabit Etherchannel or 10-Gig Ethernet, with an oversubscription of no more than 4:1.

VLAN Planning

Before beginning a VLAN implementation, you need to determine the following information:

- VLAN numbering, naming and IP addressing scheme
- VLAN placement—local or multiple switches
- Are any trunks necessary and where?
- VTP parameters
- Test and verification plan

Creating a VLAN and Assigning Ports

VLANs must be created before they can be used. Creating VLANs is easy—in global configuration mode just identify the VLAN number and optionally name it!

```
(config)# vlan 12
(config-vlan)# name MYVLAN
```

Delete a VLAN by using the same command with **no** in front of it. There is no need to include the name when deleting.

When statically assigning ports to VLANs, first make the interface an access port, and then assign the port to a VLAN. At the interface configuration prompt:

```
(config-if)# switchport mode access
(config-if)# switchport access vlan 12
```

Verifying VLAN Configuration

To see a list of all the VLANs and the ports assigned to them, use the command **show vlan**. To narrow down the information displayed, you can use these keywords after the command: **brief, id**, vlan-number, or **name** vlan-name:

```
ASW# show vlan brief
VLAN Name    Status   Ports
---- ------------------------------ --------- --------------------
    ----------
1   default  active  Fa0/1, Fa0/2, Fa0/3,
     Fa0/10,Fa0/11,Fa0/12
20  VLAN0020  active  Fa0/5,Fa0/6,Fa0/7
21  VLAN0021  active  Fa0/8,Fa0/9
1002 fddi-default  active
1003 trcrf-default  active
1004 fddinet-default  active
1005 trbrf-default  active
```

Other verification commands include

- **show running-config interface** *interface no*: Use the following to verify the VLAN membership of the port:

  ```
  ASW# show run interface fa0/5
  Building configuration...
  Current configuration 64 bytes
  interface FastEthernet 0/5
   switchport access vlan 20
   switchport mode access
  ```

- **show mac address-*table* interface** *interface-no.* **vlan** *vlan no*: Use the following to view MAC addresses learned through that port for the specified VLAN:

  ```
  ASW# show mac address-table interface fa0/1
       Mac Address Table
  -------------------------------------------
  Vlan  Mac Address   Type     Ports
  ----  -----------   ----     -----
  1    0030.b656.7c3d DYNAMIC   Fa0/1
  Total Mac Addresses for this criterion: 1
  ```

- **show interfaces** *interface-no.* **switchport:** Use the following to see detailed information about the port configuration, such as entries in the Administrative Mode and Access Mode VLAN fields:

  ```
  ASW# show interfaces fa0/1 switchport
  Name: Fa0/1
  Switchport: Enabled
  Administrative Mode: dynamic desirable
  Operational Mode: static access
  Administrative Trunking Encapsulation: negotiate
  Operational Trunking Encapsulation: native
  ```

```
Negotiation of Trunking: On
Access Mode VLAN: 1 (default)
Trunking Native Mode VLAN: 1 (default)
Trunking VLANs Enabled: ALL
Pruning VLANs Enabled: 2-1001
Protected: false
Unknown unicast blocked: false
Unknown multicast blocked: false
Broadcast Suppression Level: 100
Multicast Suppression Level: 100
Unicast Suppression Level: 100
```

VLAN Trunking

A *trunk* is a link that carries traffic for more than one VLAN. Trunks multiplex traffic from multiple VLANs. They typically connect switches and enable ports on multiple switches to be assigned to the same VLAN.

Two methods of identifying VLANs over trunk links are

- **Inter-Switch Link (ISL):** A Cisco proprietary method that encapsulates the original frame in a header, which contains VLAN information. It is protocol-independent and can identify Cisco Discovery Protocol (CDP) and bridge protocol data unit (BPDU) frames.

- **802.1Q:** Standards-based, tags the frames (inserts a field into the original frame immediately after the source MAC address field), and supports Ethernet and Token Ring networks.

When a frame comes into a switch port, the frame is tagged internally within the switch with the VLAN number of the port. When it reaches the outgoing port, the internal tag is removed. If the exit port is a trunk port, its VLAN is identified in either the ISL encapsulation or the 802.1Q tag. The switch on the other end of the trunk removes the ISL or 802.1Q information, checks the VLAN of the frame, and adds the internal tag. If the exit port is a user port, the original frame is sent out unchanged, making the use of VLANs transparent to the user.

If a nontrunking port receives an ISL-encapsulated packet, the port cannot remove the ISL header. By default, the system installs ISL system CAM entries and drops ISL packets. In special, rare circumstances, these CAM entries are installed for every active VLAN in the switch. To prevent such collisions, enter the **no-isl-entries enable** command on switches connected to other switches. If the ISL header and footer cause the MTU size to be exceeded, it might be counted as an error.

If a nontrunking port receives an 802.1Q frame, the source and destination MAC addresses are read, the tag field is ignored, and the frame is switched normally at Layer 2.

Configuring a Trunk Link

Ports can become trunk ports either by static configuration or dynamic negotiation using Dynamic Trunking Protocol (DTP). A switch port can be in one of five DTP modes:

- **Access:** The port is a user port in a single VLAN.

- **Trunk:** The port negotiates trunking with the port on the other end of the link.

- **Non-negotiate:** The port is a trunk and does not do DTP negotiation with the other side of the link.

- **Dynamic Desirable:** Actively negotiates trunking with the other side of the link. It becomes a trunk if the port on the other switch is set to **trunk**, **dynamic desirable**, or **dynamic auto** mode.

- **Dynamic Auto:** Passively waits to be contacted by the other switch. It becomes a trunk if the other end is set to **trunk** or **dynamic desirable** mode.

Configure a port for trunking at the interface configuration mode:

```
(config-if)#switchport mode {dynamic {auto | desirable} | trunk}
```

If dynamic mode is used, DTP negotiates the trunking state and encapsulation. If trunk mode is used, you must specify encapsulation, and you can disable all DTP negotiation:

```
(config-if)#switchport trunk encapsulation {isl | dot1q | negotiate}
(config-if)# switchport nonnegotiate
```

If you use 802.1Q, specify a native VLAN for the trunk link with the command:

```
(config-if)# switchport trunk native vlan vlan-no
```

Frames from the native VLAN are sent over the trunk link untagged. Native VLAN must match on both sides of the trunk link. VLAN 1 is the default native VLAN for all ports, but best practice is to set the native VLAN to one not assigned to users. This practice also decreases the danger of having a large spanning tree instance in VLAN1.

VLANs Allowed on the Trunk

By default, a trunk carries traffic for all VLANs. You can change that behavior for a particular trunk link by giving the following command at the interface config mode:

```
switchport trunk allowed vlan vlans
```

Make sure that both sides of a trunk link enable the same VLANs.

Verifying a Trunk Link

Two commands you can use to verify your trunk configuration are

```
# show running-config
# show interfaces [interface no.] switchport | trunk
```

Using the **trunk** keyword with the **show interfaces** command gives information about the trunk link:

```
# show interfaces fastethernet 0/1 trunk
Port    Mode      Encapsulation Status     Native vlan
Fa0/1   desirable  n-802.1q      trunking   1
Port    Vlans allowed on trunk
Fa0/1   1-150
<further output omitted>
```

Best Practices for Trunking

- Change the Native VLAN to one not assigned to any users.

- On links that should be trunks, turn off trunking negotiation by setting the mode to **trunk**, specifying the encapsulation type, and adding the **nonnegotiate** command.

- On links that should never be trunks, turn off trunking negotiation by setting the switchport mode to **host**. This sets it as an access port, enables Portfast, and disables EtherChannel negotiation.

- Limit the VLAN traffic carried by the trunk to only those VLANs it needs to carry.

VLAN Trunking Protocol

VLAN Trunking Protocol (VTP) is a Cisco-proprietary protocol that runs over trunk links and synchronizes the VLAN databases of all switches in the

VTP domain. A VTP domain is an administrative group; all switches within that group must have the same VTP domain name configured, or they do not synchronize databases.

VTP works by using Configuration Revision numbers and VTP advertisements:

- All switches send out VTP advertisements every five minutes or when there is a change to the VLAN database (when a VLAN is created, deleted, or renamed).

- VTP advertisements contain a Configuration Revision number. This number is increased by one for every VLAN change.

- When a switch receives a VTP advertisement, it compares the Configuration Revision number against the one in its VLAN database.

- If the new number is higher, the switch overwrites its database with the new VLAN information and forwards the information to its neighbor switches.

- If the number is the same, the switch ignores the advertisement.

- If the new number is lower, the switch replies with the more up-to-date information contained in its own database.

VTP Switch Roles

A switch can be a VTP:

- **Server:** The default VTP role. Servers can create, delete, and rename VLANs. They originate both periodic and triggered VTP advertisements and synchronize their databases with other switches in the domain.

- **Client:** Clients cannot make VLAN changes. They originate periodic VTP advertisements and synchronize their databases with other switches in the domain.

- **Transparent:** It can create, delete, and rename VLANs, but its VLANs are only local. It does not originate advertisements or synchronize its database with any other switches. It forwards VTP advertisements out its trunk links, however.

The two versions of VTP are Version 1 and Version 2. To use Version 2, all switches in the domain must be capable of using it. Configure one server for

Version 2, and the information is propagated through VTP. Version 2 has the following added features:

- It supports Token Ring VLANs.

- Transparent switches pass along messages from both versions of VTP.

- Consistency checks are performed only when changes are configured through the CLI or SNMP.

Configuring VTP

VTP configuration is done at the global config mode. To configure the switch's VTP mode:

```
(config)# vtp {server | client |transparent}
```

To configure the VTP domain name:

```
(config)# vtp domain name
```

To configure a VTP password (all switches in the domain must use the same password):

```
(config)# vtp password password
```

To configure the switch to use VTP Version 2:

```
(config)# vtp version 2
```

Verifying and Monitoring VTP

To get basic information about the VTP configuration, use **show vtp status**. The example shows the default settings:

```
# show vtp status
VTP Version  : 1
Configuration Revision  : 0
Maximum VLANs supported locally  : 1005
Number of existing VLANs  : 5
VTP Operating Mode  : Server
VTP Domain Name  :
(config)#
VTP Pruning Mode  : Disabled
VTP V2 Mode  : Disabled
VTP Traps Generation  : Disabled
MD5 digest  :
```

Adding a New Switch to a VTP Domain

Adding a new switch in client mode does not prevent it from propagating its incorrect VLAN information. A server synchronizes to a client if the client has the higher configuration revision number. You must reset the revision number back to 0 on the new switch. To be safe, follow these steps:

1. With the switch disconnected from the network, set it as VTP transparent and delete the vlan.dat file from its flash memory.

2. Set it to a fake VTP domain name and into client mode.

3. Reboot the switch.

4. Configure the correct VTP settings, such as domain, password, mode, and version.

5. Connect the switch to the network, and verify that it receives the correct information.

EtherChannels

An EtherChannel is a way of combining several physical links between switches into one logical connection. Normally, Spanning Tree blocks redundant links; EtherChannels get around that and enable load balancing across those links. Traffic is balanced between the channel links on the basis of such things as source or destination MAC address or IP address. The EtherChannel load-balancing method is configured at global configuration mode.

```
(config)# port-channel load-balance type
```

A logical interface—called the Port Channel interface—is created. Configuration can be applied to both the logical and physical interfaces.

Some guidelines for EtherChannels follows:

- Interfaces in the channel do not have to be physically next to each other or on the same module.

- All ports must be the same speed and duplex.

- All ports in the bundle should be enabled.

- None of the bundle ports can be a SPAN port.

- Assign an IP address to the logical Port Channel interface, not the physical ones, if using a Layer 3 EtherChannel.

- Put all bundle ports in the same VLAN, or make them all trunks. If they are trunks, they must all carry the same VLANs and use the same trunking mode.

- The configuration you apply to the Port Channel interface affects the entire EtherChannel. The configuration you apply to a physical interface affects only that interface.

Configuring an EtherChannel

Basically, you should configure the logical interface and then put the physical interfaces into the channel group:

```
(config)# interface port-channel number
![any additional configuration, such as trunking for a Layer 2
 EtherChannel]
```

For a Layer 3 EtherChannel, add the following:

```
(config-if)# no switchport
(config-if)# ip address address mask
```

Then, at each port that is part of the EtherChannel, use the following:

```
(config)# interface { number | range interface - interface}
(config-if)# channel-group number mode {auto | desirable | on}
```

Putting the IP address on the Port Channel interface creates a Layer 3 EtherChannel. Simply putting interfaces into a channel group creates a Layer 2 EtherChannel, and the logical interface is automatically created.

The Cisco proprietary Port Aggregation Protocol (PAgP) dynamically negotiates the formation of a channel. There are three PAgP modes:

- **On:** The port channels without using PAgP negotiation. The port on the other side must also be set to On.

- **Auto:** Responds to PAgP messages but does not initiate them. Port channels if the port on the other end is set to Desirable. This is the default mode.

- **Desirable:** Port actively negotiates channeling status with the interface on the other end of the link. Port channels if the other side is Auto or Desirable.

Link Aggregation Control Protocol (LACP) is an IEEE standard protocol, IEEE 802.3ad, which does the same thing. LACP modes follow:

- **On:** The port channels without using LACP negotiation. The port on the other side must also be set to On.

- **Active:** Port actively negotiates channeling with the port on the other end of the link. A channel forms if the other side is Passive or Active.

- **Passive:** Responds to LACP messages but does not initiate them. A channel forms only if the other end is set to Active.

If you want to use LACP, specify it under the interface and put the interface in either active or passive mode:

```
(config-if)# channel-protocol lacp
(config-if)channel-group number mode {active/passive}
```

Verifying an EtherChannel

Some typical commands for verifying include the following:

```
# show running-config interface number
# show interfaces number etherchannel
# show etherchannel number port-channel
# show etherchannel summary
# show etherchannel load-balance
```

Troubleshooting VLAN Issues

Configuration problems can arise when user traffic must traverse several switches. The following sections list some common configuration errors. But before you begin troubleshooting, create a plan. Check the implementation plan for any changes recently made, and determine likely problem areas.

Troubleshooting User Connectivity

User connectivity can be affected by several things:

- **Physical connectivity:** Make sure the cable, network adapter, and switch port are good. Check the port's link LED.

- **Switch configuration:** If you see FCS errors or late collisions, suspect a duplex mismatch. Check configured speed on both sides of the link. Make sure the port is enabled and set as an access port.

- **VLAN configuration:** Make sure the hosts are in the correct VLAN.

- **Allowed VLANs:** Make sure that the user VLAN is allowed on all appropriate trunk links.

Troubleshooting Trunking

When troubleshooting trunking, make sure that physical layer connectivity is present before moving on to search for configuration problems such as

- Are both sides of the link in the correct trunking mode?

- Is the same trunk encapsulation on both sides?

- If 802.1Q, is the same native VLAN on both sides? Look for CDP messages warning of this error.

- Are the same VLANs permitted on both sides?

- Is a link trunking that should not be?

Troubleshooting VTP

The following are some common things to check when troubleshooting problems with VTP:

- Make sure you are trunking between the switches. VTP is sent only over trunk links.

- Make sure the domain name matches on both switches. (The name is case sensitive.)

- If the switch is not updating its database, make sure it is not in transparent mode.

- If using passwords, make sure they all match. To remove a password, use **no vtp password**.

- If VLANs are missing, check the Revision number for a possible database overwrite. Also check the number of VLANs in the domain. There might be too many VLANs for VTP to update properly.

## CHAPTER 3

Spanning Tree

Ethernet network design balances two separate imperatives. First, Ethernet has no capacity for detecting circular paths. If such paths exist, traffic loops around and accumulates until new traffic is shut out. (This is called a broadcast storm.) Second, having secondary paths is good preparation for inevitable link failure.

Spanning Tree is a protocol that prevents loop formation by detecting redundant links and disabling them until needed. Designers can therefore build redundant links, and the protocol enables one to pass traffic and keep the other in reserve. When the active link fails, the secondary link is enabled quickly.

Understanding the Spanning Tree Protocol

Switches either forward or filter Layer 2 frames. The way they make the forwarding/filtering decision can lead to loops in a network with redundant links. Spanning Tree is a protocol that detects potential loops and breaks them.

A Layer 2 switch is functionally the same thing as a transparent bridge. Transparent bridges:

- Learn MAC (Media Access Control) addresses by looking at the source address of incoming frames. They build a table mapping MAC address to port number.

- Forward broadcasts and multicasts out all ports except the one which they came. (This is called flooding.)

- Forward unknown unicasts out all ports except the one in which they came. An unknown unicast is a message bound for a unicast MAC address that is not in the switch's table of addresses and ports.

- Do not make any changes to the frames as they forward them.

Spanning Tree Protocol (STP) works by selecting a root bridge and then selecting one loop-free path from the root bridge to every other switch. (STP

uses the term *bridge* because it was written before there were switches.)
Consider the following switched network (see Figure 3-1).

Figure 3-1   Example Switched Topology

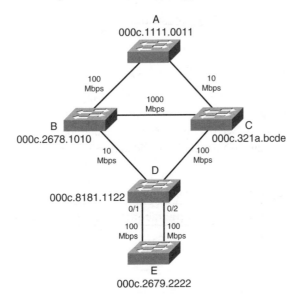

Spanning Tree must select

- One root bridge

- One root port per nonroot bridge

- One designated port per network segment

Spanning Tree Election Criteria

Spanning Tree builds paths out from a central point along the fastest available links. It selects paths according to the following criteria:

- Lowest root bridge ID (BID)

- Lowest path cost to the root

- Lowest sender bridge ID

- Lowest sender port ID (PID)

When reading the path selection criteria, remember the following:

- **Bridge ID:** Bridge priority: Bridge MAC address.

- **Bridge priority:** 2-btye value, 0–65,535 (0–0xFFFF).

- **Default priority:** 32,768 (0x8000).

- **Port ID:** Port priority: port number.

- **Port priority:** A 6-bit value, 0–63, default is 32.

- **Path cost:** This is the cumulative value of the cost of each link between the bridge and the root. Cost values were updated in 2000, and you should see only new cost values, but both are given in the following table (see Table 3-1). Old and new switches work together.

Table 3-1   Spanning Tree Costs

Link Speed	Previous IEEE Specification	Current IEEE Specification
10 Mb/s	100	100
100 Mb/s	10	19
1 Gbps	1	4
10 Gbps	1	2

STP Election

Spanning Tree builds paths out from a starting point, the "root" of the tree. The first step in selecting paths is to identify this root device. Then each device selects its best path back to the root, according to the criteria laid out in the previous sections (lowest root BID, lowest cost, lowest advertising BID, lowest port ID).

Root Bridge Election

Looking at Figure 3-1, first select the root bridge. Assume each switch uses the default priority.

- Switch A BID = 80–00–00–0c-11–11–00–11

- Switch B BID = 80–00–00–0c–26–78–10–10

- Switch C BID = 80–00–00–0c-32–1a-bc-de

- Switch D BID = 80–00–00–0c-81–81–11–22

- Switch E BID = 80–00–00–0c–26–79–22–22

Switch A has the lowest BID, so it is the root. Each nonroot switch must now select a root port.

Root Port Election

The root port is the port that leads back to the root. Continuing with Figure 3-1, when A is acknowledged as the root, the remaining bridges sort out their lowest cost path back to the A:

- **Switch B:** Uses the link to A with a cost of 19 (link speed of 100 Mb/s).

- **Switch C:** The connected link has a cost of 100 (Ethernet), the link through B has a path cost of 38 (two 100-Mb/s links), and so B is chosen.

- **Switch D:** The link through B has a path cost of 119, the path cost through C to A is 119, the path through C then B is 57, so C is chosen.

- **Switch E:** The lowest path cost is the same for both ports (76 through D to C to B to A). Next check sender BID—sender for both ports is D so that it does not break the tie. Next check sender Port ID. Assuming default port priority, the PID for 0/1 is lower than the PID for 0/2, so the port on the left is the root port.

Designated Port Election

Designated ports are ports that lead away from the root. Obviously, all ports on the root bridge are designated ports (A–B and A–C in Figure 3-1).

- **Segment B–D:** B has the lowest path cost to root (19 versus 119), so it is designated for this segment.

- **Segment C–D:** C has the lowest path cost to the root (100 versus 119), so it is designated for this segment.

- **Segment B–C:** B has the lowest path cost to the root (19 versus 100), so it is designated for this segment.

- **Both segments D–E:** D has the lowest cost to the root (57 versus 76), so it is designated for both segments.

Now the looped topology has been turned into a tree with A at the root. Notice that there are no more redundant links.

Figure 3-2 Active Topology After Spanning Tree Is Complete

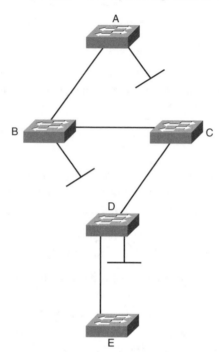

Bridge Protocol Data Units

Switches exchange Bridge Protocol Data Units (BPDU). The two types of BPDUs are Configuration and Topology Change Notification(TCN). Configuration BPDUs are sent every two seconds from the root toward the downstream switches. They:

- Are used during an election

- Maintain connectivity between switches

- Send timer information from the root

TCN BPDUs are sent by a downstream switch toward the root when:

- There is a link failure.

- A port starts forwarding, and there is already a designated port.

- The switch receives a TCN from a neighbor.

When a switch receives a TCN BPDU, it acknowledges that with a configuration BPDU that has the TCN Acknowledgment bit set.

When the root bridge receives a TCN, it starts sending configuration BPDUs with the TCN bit set for a period of time equal to max age plus forward delay. Switches that receive this change their MAC table aging time to the Forward Delay time, causing MAC addresses to age faster. The topology change also causes an election of the root bridge, root ports, and designated ports.

Some of the fields in the BPDU include

- **Root bridge ID:** The BID of the current root

- **Sender's root path cost:** The cost to the root

- **Sender's bridge ID:** Sender's priority concatenated to MAC

- **Sender's port ID:** The port number, transmitted as final tie-breaker

- **Hello time:** Two seconds by default

- **Forward Delay:** Fifteen seconds by default

- **Max Age:** Twenty seconds by default

Spanning Tree Port States

When a port is first activated, it transitions through the following stages shown in Table 3-2.

Table 3-2   Spanning Tree Port States

Port State	Timer	Action
Blocking	Max Age (20 sec)	Discards frames, does not learn MAC addresses, receives BPDUs
Listening	Forward Delay (15 sec)	Discards frames, does not learn MAC addresses, receives BPDUs to determine its role in the network
Learning	Forward Delay (15 sec)	Discards frames, does learn MAC addresses, receives and transmits BPDUs
Forwarding		Accepts frames, learns MAC addresses, receives and transmits BPDUs

Per-VLAN Spanning-Tree

The IEEE's version of STP assumes one common Spanning-tree instance (and thus one root bridge) regardless of how many VLANs are configured.

With the Cisco Per-VLAN Spanning-Tree (PVST+) there is a different instance of STP for each VLAN. To derive the VLAN BID, the switch picks a different MAC address from its base pool for each VLAN. Each VLAN has its own root bridge, root port, and so on. You can configure these so that data flow is optimized, and traffic load is balanced among the switches by configuring different root bridges for groups of VLANs.

PVST+ is enabled by default on Cisco switches.

Configuring Spanning Tree

To change the STP priority value, use the following:

```
Switch (config)# spanning-tree vlan vlan_no. priority value
```

To configure a switch as root without manually changing priority values, use the following:

```
Switch (config)# spanning-tree vlan vlan_no. root {primary | secondary}
```

To change the STP port cost for an access port, use the following:

```
Switch(config-if)# spanning-tree cost value
```

To change the STP port cost for a VLAN on a trunk port, use the following:

```
Switch(config-if)# spanning-tree vlan vlan_no. cost value
```

To display STP information for a VLAN, use the following:

```
Switch# show spanning-tree vlan vlan_no.
```

To display the STP information for an interface, use the following:

```
Switch # show spanning-tree interface interface_no. [detail]
```

To verify STP timers, use the following:

```
Switch # show spanning-tree bridge brief
```

Portfast

Portfast is a Cisco-proprietary enhancement to Spanning Tree that helps speed up network convergence. It is for access (user) ports only. Portfast causes the port to transition directly to forwarding, bypassing the other STP states. Connecting a switch to a Portfast port can cause loops to develop. Configure Portfast on an interface or interface range:

```
(config-if)# spanning-tree portfast
```

It can also be configured globally:

```
(config)# spanning-tree portfast default
```

Rapid Spanning Tree

Rapid Spanning Tree (RSTP) 802.1w is a standards-based, nonproprietary way of speeding STP convergence. Switch ports exchange an explicit handshake when they transition to forwarding. RSTP describes different port states than regular STP, as shown in Table 3-3.

Table 3-3   Comparing 802.1d and 802.1w Port States

STP Port State	Equivalent RSTP Port State
Disabled	Discarding
Blocking	Discarding
Listening	Discarding
Learning	Learning
Forwarding	Forwarding

RSTP Port Roles

RSTP also defines different Spanning Tree roles for ports:

- **Root port:** The best path to the root (same as STP)

- **Designated port:** Same role as with STP

- **Alternate port:** A backup to the root port

- **Backup port:** A backup to the designated port

- **Disabled port:** Not used in the Spanning Tree

- **Edge port:** Connected only to an end user

BPDU Differences in RSTP

In regular STP, BPDUs are originated by the root and relayed by each switch. In RSTP, each switch originates BPDUs, whether or not it receives a BPDU on its root port. All eight bits of the BPDU type field are used by RSTP. The TC and TC Ack bits are still used. The other six bits specify the port's role and its RSTP state and are used in the port handshake. The RSTP

BPDU is set to Type 2, Version 2. PVST is done by Rapid PVST+ on Catalyst switches.

RSTP Fast Convergence

The Rapid Spanning Tree process understands and incorporates topology changes much quicker than the previous version:

- **RSTP uses a mechanism similar to BackboneFast:** When an inferior BPDU is received, the switch accepts it. If the switch has another path to the root, it uses that and informs its downstream switch of the alternative path.

- **Edge ports work the same as Portfast ports:** They automatically transition directly to forwarding.

- **Link type:** If you connect two switches through a point-to-point link and the local port becomes a designated port, it exchanges a handshake with the other port to quickly transition to forwarding. Full-duplex links are assumed to be point-to-point; half-duplex links are assumed to be shared.

- **Backup and alternate ports:** Ports that can transition to forwarding when no BPDUs are received from a neighbor switch (similar to UplinkFast).

If an RSTP switch detects a topology change, it sets a TC timer to twice the hello time and sets the TC bit on all BPDUs sent out its designated and root ports until the timer expires. It also clears the MAC addresses learned on these ports. Only changes to the status of non-Edge ports cause a TC notification.

If an RSTP switch receives a TC BPDU, it clears the MAC addresses on that port and sets the TC bit on all BPDUs sent out its designated and root ports until the TC timer expires. Enable and verify Rapid STP with the commands:

```
Switch(config)# spanning-tree mode rapid-pvst
Switch# show spanning-tree
```

A version of PVST+ is used with Rapid Spanning Tree, called Per-VLAN Rapid Spanning Tree (PVRST+). You should still configure root and secondary root bridges for each VLAN when using RSTP.

Multiple Spanning Tree

With Multiple Spanning Tree (MST), you can group VLANs and run one instance of Spanning Tree for a group of VLANs. This cuts down on the number of root bridges, root ports, designated ports, and BPDUs in your network. Switches in the same MST Region share the same configuration and VLAN mappings. Configure and verify MST with these commands:

```
(config)# spanning-tree mode mst
(config)# spanning-tree mst configuration
(config-mst)# name region_name
(config-mst)# revision number
(config-mst)# instance number vlan vlan_range
(config-mst)# end
# show spanning-tree mst
```

To be compatible with 802.1Q trunking, which has one common Spanning Tree (CST) for all VLANs, MST runs one instance of an Internal Spanning Tree (IST). The IST appears as one bridge to a CST area and is MST instance number 0. The original MST Spanning Trees (called M-Trees) are active only in the region; they combine at the edge of the CST area to form one.

Spanning Tree Stability Mechanisms

Spanning Tree has several additional tools for tuning STP to protect the network and keep it operating properly. They include

- PortFast (discussed previously)
- UplinkFast
- BackboneFast
- BPDU Guard
- BPDU Filtering
- Root Guard
- UDLD
- Loop Guard

UplinkFast

UplinkFast is for speeding convergence when a direct link to an upstream switch fails. The switch identifies backup ports for the root port. (These are called an uplink group.) If the root port fails, one of the ports in the uplink group is unblocked and transitions immediately to forwarding; it bypasses the listening and learning stages. It should be used in wiring closet switches with at least one blocked port.

The command to enable uplinkfast is shown next. Please note that uplinkfast is enabled globally, so the command affects all ports and all VLANs.

```
(config)# spanning-tree uplinkfast
```

BackboneFast

BackboneFast is used for speeding convergence when a link fails that is not directly connected to the switch. It helps the switch detect indirect failures. If a switch running BackboneFast receives an inferior BPDU from its desig-nated bridge, it knows a link on the path to the root has failed. (An inferior BPDU is one that lists the same switch for the root bridge and designated bridge.)

The switch then tries to find an alternate path to the root by sending a Root Link Query (RLQ) frame out all alternate ports. The root then responds with an RLQ response, and the port receiving this response can transition to forwarding. Alternate ports are determined in this way:

- If the inferior BPDU was received on a blocked port, the root port and any other blocked ports are considered alternates.

- If the inferior BPDU was received on the root port, all blocked ports are considered alternates.

- If the inferior BPDU was received on the root port and there are no blocked ports, the switch assumes it has lost connectivity with the root and advertises itself as root.

Configure this command on all switches in the network:

```
(config)# spanning-tree backbonefast
```

BPDU Guard

BPDU Guard prevents loops if another switch is attached to a Portfast port. When BPDU Guard is enabled on an interface, it is put into an error-disabled state (basically, shut down) if a BPDU is received on the interface. It can be enabled at either global config mode—in which case it affects all Portfast interfaces—or at interface mode. Portfast does not need to be enabled for it to be configured at a specific interface. The following configuration example shows BPDU guard being enabled and verified.

```
(config)# spanning-tree portfast bpduguard default
(config-if)# spanning-tree bpduguard enable
# show spanning-tree summary totals
```

BPDU Filtering

BPDU filtering is another way of preventing loops in the network. It also can be enabled either globally or at the interface and functions differently at each. In global config, if a Portfast interface receives any BPDUs, it is taken out of Portfast status. At interface config mode, it prevents the port from sending or receiving BPDUs. The commands are

```
(config)# spanning-tree portfast bpdufilter default
(config-if)# spanning-tree bpdufilter enable
```

Root Guard

Root Guard is meant to prevent the wrong switch from becoming the Spanning Tree root. It is enabled on ports other than the root port and on switches other than the root. If a Root Guard port receives a BPDU that might cause it to become a root port, the port is put into "root-inconsistent" state and does not pass traffic through it. If the port stops receiving these BPDUs, it automatically reenables itself. To enable and verify Root Guard use the following commands:

```
(config-if)# spanning-tree guard root
# show spanning-tree inconsistentports
```

Unidirectional Link Detection

A switch notices when a physical connection is broken by the absence of Layer 1 electrical keepalives. (Ethernet calls this a link beat.) However, sometimes a cable is intact enough to maintain keepalives but not to pass data in both directions. This is a Unidirectional Link. Operating at Layer 2, Unidirectional Link Detection (UDLD) detects a unidirectional link by sending periodic hellos out to the interface. It also uses probes, which must be acknowledged by the device on the other end of the link.

UDLD has two modes: normal and aggressive. In normal mode, the link status is changed to Undetermined State if the hellos are not returned. In aggressive mode, the port is error-disabled if a unidirectional link is found. Aggressive mode is the recommended way to configure UDLD.

To enable UDLD on all fiber-optic interfaces, use the following command:

```
(config)# udld [enable | aggressive]
```

Although this command is given at global config mode, it applies only to fiber ports.

To enable UDLD on nonfiber ports, give the same command at interface config mode.

To control UDLD on a specific fiber port, use the following command:

```
(config-if)# udld port {aggressive | disable}
```

To reenable all interfaces shut by UDLD, use the following:

```
# udld reset
```

To verify UDLD status, use the following:

```
# show udld interface
```

Loop Guard

Loop Guard prevents loops that might develop if a port that should be blocking inadvertently transitions to the forwarding state. This can happen if the port stops receiving BPDUs (perhaps because of a unidirectional link or a software/configuration problem in its neighbor switch). When one of the ports in a physically redundant topology stops receiving BPDUs, the STP conceives the topology as loop-free. Eventually, the blocking port becomes designated and moves to forwarding state, thus creating a loop. With Loop Guard enabled, an additional check is made.

If no BPDUs are received on a blocked port for a specific length of time, Loop Guard puts that port into "loop inconsistent" blocking state, rather than transitioning to forwarding state. Loop Guard should be enabled on all switch ports that have a chance of becoming root or designated ports. It is most effective when enabled in the entire switched network in conjunction with UDLD.

To enable Loop Guard for all point-to-point links on the switch, use the following command:

```
(config)# spanning-tree loopguard default
```

To enable Loop Guard on a specific interface, use the following:

`(config-if)# ` **`spanning-tree guard loop`**

Loop Guard automatically reenables the port if it starts receiving BPDUs again.

Troubleshooting STP

Some common things to look for when troubleshooting Spanning Tree Protocol include

- **Duplex mismatch:** When one side of a link is half-duplex and the other is full-duplex. This causes late collisions and FCS errors.

- **Unidirectional link failure:** The link is up but data flows only in one direction. It can cause loops.

- **Frame corruption:** Physical errors on the line cause BPDUs to be lost, and the port incorrectly begins forwarding. This is caused by duplex mismatch, bad cable, or cable too long.

- **Resource errors:** STP is implemented in software, so a switch with an overloaded CPU or memory might neglect some STP duties.

- **Port Fast configuration errors:** Connecting a switch to two ports that have Port Fast enabled. This can cause a loop.

- **STP tuning errors:** Max age or forward delay set too short can cause a loop. A network diameter that is set too low causes BPDUs to be discarded and affects STP convergence.

Identifying a Bridging Loop

Suspect a loop if you see the following:

- You capture traffic on a link and see the same frames multiple times.

- All users in a bridging domain have connectivity problems at the same time.

- There is abnormally high port utilization.

To remedy a loop quickly, shut redundant ports and then enable them one at a time. Some switches enable debugging of STP to help in diagnosing problems. The following commands are useful for isolating a bridging loop:

> **show interfaces**
>
> **show spanning tree**
>
> **show bridge**
>
> **show process cpu**
>
> **debug spanning tree**
>
> **show mac address-table aging-time** *vlan#*
>
> **show spanning-tree vlan** *vlan#* **detail**

Spanning-Tree Best Practices

To optimize data flow in the network, design and configure Spanning Tree in the following ways:

- Statically configure switches to be the primary and secondary root bridges by setting priority values.

- Consider which interfaces will become designated and root ports (possibly set port priorities/path cost).

- Tune STP using the tools detailed in this section.

- Enable UDLD aggressive mode on all fiber interfaces.

- Design STP domains that are as simple and contained as possible by using multilayer switches and routed links.

- Use PVRST+ or MST for the fastest convergence times.

Confused by all the acronyms and STP features? Figure 3-3 shows the STP tools you might use in your network and where you might use them.

Figure 3-3   Example Switched Topology

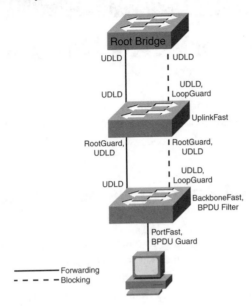

## CHAPTER 4

InterVLAN Routing

VLANs divide the network into smaller broadcast domains but also prohibit communication between domains. To enable communication between those groups–without also passing broadcasts–routing is used.

InterVLAN Routing Using an External Router

A Layer 2 switch can connect to a router to provide reachability between VLANs. This can be done either via separate physical links for each VLAN or via a trunk link from the switch to the router. A trunk link is most common and this type of setup is frequently called Router on a Stick.

When using a trunk link you must create separate subinterfaces on the router's physical interface—one subinterface for each VLAN plus one for the native VLAN. This can work with any kind of switch and the implementation is straightforward, but the router becomes a single point of failure for all users, and the trunk link might become congested.

The router's configuration would look similar to the following:

```
interface FastEthernet0/1
 no ip address
 duplex auto
 speed auto
!
interface FastEthernet0/1.20
 description Voice VLAN
 encapsulation dot1Q 20
 ip address 10.1.20.1 255.255.255.0
!
interface FastEthernet0/1.99
 description Native VLAN
 encapsulation dot1Q 99 native
 ip address 10.1.99.1 255.255.255.0
!
interface FastEthernet0/1.120
 description Data VLAN
 encapsulation dot1Q 120
 ip address 10.1.120.1.255.255.255.0
```

InterVLAN Routing Using Multilayer Switches

A multilayer switch can do both Layer 2 switching and Layer 3 routing between VLANs. This section walks you through the switching process and focuses on order of operations. The order in which things happen is extremely important for two reasons. First, the order of events is good test material. Second, understanding the processing order allows you to evaluate how the various filtering and forwarding mechanisms interact. (Examples include error checking, access-lists, VLAN access-lists, routing, and QoS.)

The Layer 2 and Layer 3 Forwarding Process

A multilayer switch does Layer 2 forwarding when the destination MAC address is mapped to one of its interfaces. The steps involved in Layer 2 forwarding are as follows:

Input

1. Receive frame

2. Verify frame integrity

3. Apply inbound VLAN ACL (VLAN Access Control List)

4. Look up destination MAC (Media Address Code)

Output

1. Apply outbound VLAN ACL

2. Apply outbound QoS ACL

3. Select output port

4. Place in port queue

5. Rewrite

6. Forward

A multilayer switch does Layer 3 forwarding when the destination MAC address is one of the switch's own addresses. The steps involved in Layer 3 forwarding are as follows:

Input

1. Receive frame.

2. Verify frame integrity.

3. Apply inbound VLAN ACL.

4. Look up destination MAC.

Routing

1. Apply input ACL

2. Switch if entry is in CEF cache

3. Apply output ACL

Output

1. Apply outbound VLAN ACL.

2. Apply outbound QoS ACL.

3. Select output port.

4. Place in interface queue.

5. Rewrite source and destination MAC, IP checksum and frame check sequence, and decrement TTL (Time to Live field in the IP header).

6. Forward.

Understanding the Switching Table

Multilayer switches use Application Specific Integrated Circuits (ASIC) to forward packets at wire speed. The Content Addressable Memory (CAM) table, used for Layer 2 switching, is created by recording the source MAC address and ingress port of each frame. It contains binary values (0 or 1) and must find an exact match to have a hit.

In comparison, Multilayer Switching (MLS) uses aa Ternary Content Addressable Memory (TCAM) table to store information needed by Layer 3 and higher processing. This might include QoS and ACLs. Values in the TCAM table include ternary values (0, 1, or wildcard). An exact match is not required—the longest match is considered a hit.

MLS Interfaces

A multilayer switch can have the following types of interfaces:

- **Layer 2 Interface:** Either an access port assigned to a VLAN or a trunk port.

- **Switch Virtual Interface (SVI):** A virtual, software interface for the VLAN itself. Can be either a Layer 2 interface or a Layer 3 interface.

- **Routed Interface:** A physical interface that is not associated with a VLAN and acts like a router port.

SVI Configuration

A default SVI for VLAN 1 is automatically created in the switch. To create an SVI use the command **interface** *vlan#*. Configure an IP address on the SVI to make it a Layer 3 interface. SVIs are used to

- Route or fallback bridge between VLANs.

- Provide a default gateway for users in that VLAN.

- Route traffic into or out of its associated VLAN.

- Provide an IP address for connectivity to the switch itself.

- Provide an interface for routing protocols.

An SVI is considered "up" as long as at least one port in its associated VLAN is active and forwarding. If all ports in the VLAN are down, the interface goes down to avoid creating a routing black hole. You might not want the status of a particular port (one not connected to a host) to affect the SVI's status. Some Cisco switches enable you to use the following command on that interface.

```
Switch(config-if)# switchport autostate exclude
```

To configure InterVLAN routing using a Layer 3 SVI, you need to

- Enable IP routing.

- Create the VLANs.

- Create the SVIs.

- Associate an IP address with each SVI.

- Configure a dynamic routing protocol if needed.

```
Switch(config)#ip routing
Switch(config)# vlan 3
Switch(config)# interface vlan 3
Switch(config-if)#ip address 10.3.3.3 255.255.255.0
```

Routed Switch Port Configuration

To configure an interface as a routed port, you must remove the Layer 2 functionality with the **no switchport** interface command. Then you can add an IP address and configure routing as needed:

```
sw1(config)# int fa 1/0/5
sw1(config-if)# no switchport
sw1(config-if)# ip address 10.5.5.5 255.255.255.0
```

To verify your configuration, use the commands **show ip interface brief**, **show interface**, or **show running-config interface** *int-#*.

Understanding Switch Forwarding Architectures

Packets entering a router or multilayer switch are handled by one of three types of switching:

- **Process Switching:** Each packet must be examined by the CPU and handled in software. Slowest method, used in routers only.

- **Fast Switching:** CPU process switches the first packet in each flow, then caches that information, and switches subsequent packets in hardware. Faster than process switching, used in routers and multilayer switches. Also called route caching.

- **Cisco Express Forwarding (CEF):** A table is prebuilt with adjacency information for all destinations in the routing table. Fastest method, is the default for Cisco routers and multilayer switches. Also called topology-based switching.

CEF Switching

Multilayer Switching (MLS) is a switch feature that enables the switch to route traffic between VLANs and routed interfaces in a highly optimized and efficient manner. Cisco Express Forwarding (CEF) is used to facilitate MLS (see Figure 4-1). Cisco Express Forwarding (CEF) does the following:

- Separates control plane hardware from data plane hardware.

- Controls plane runs in software and builds FIB and adjacency table.

- The data plane uses hardware to forward most IP unicast traffic.

- Uses TCAM table.

- Can be centralized or distributed.

Figure 4-1   Cisco Express Forwarding

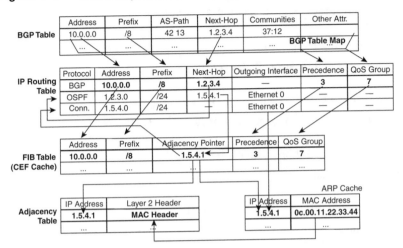

Not all types of traffic can be handled by CEF. Some types that are *punted* (sent to the processor for handling) are

- Packets with IP header options

- Tunneled traffic

- 802.3 (IPX) or other unsupported encapsulation types

- Packets with an expiring TTL

- Packets that must be fragmented

Configuring and Troubleshooting CEF

By default, CEF is on and supports per destination load sharing.

To disable CEF

- **4500:** Use (config)# `no ip cef`.

- **3500/3700:** On each interface, use (config)# `no ip route-cache cef`.

- 6550 with policy feature card, distributed FC, and multilayer switch FC: cannot be disabled.

View CEF information with the following:

`# show interface fastethernet 2/2 | begin L3`

View switching statistics with the following:

```
# show interface fastethernet 2/2 | include switched
```

View FIB with the following:

```
# show ip cef {interface} {detail}
```

View detailed CEF FIB entry with the following:

```
# show ip cef fastethernet 2/2 10.0.0.1 detail
```

Troubleshoot CEF drops with the following:

```
# show cef drop
```

Troubleshoot CEF adjacencies with the following:

```
# show adjacency
```

## CHAPTER 5

Implementing High Availability

A highly available network is the goal of every network engineer. Having a highly available network makes the job easier because it helps to prevent network outages and minimize downtime.

Components of High Availability

There are five components to high availability: redundancy, technology, people, processes, and tools. The first two can be obtained through network design; the last three are more difficult to implement and control.

Redundancy

Redundancy attempts to eliminate single points of failure by providing duplicate devices and links. This costs more, so the added cost must be balanced against the added benefit. Add redundancy where it will have the most impact on availability, in the core of your network, data center, or e-commerce module. Critical WAN or ISP connections are another possible location.

A redundant network has *path diversity* with multiple links between multiple devices. It can have *geographic diversity*, with data centers in multiple sites. Networks frequently have dual core and distribution switches, with dual uplinks to each. Dual WAN providers, with dual WAN edge routers, are commonly used. Companies can design their networks with connections to dual Telco central offices and power substations to achieve additional redundancy.

Technology

Some of the technologies found in Cisco routers and Layer 3 switches enhance availability by providing routing continuity, fast failure detection to trigger a failover, and fast routing convergence. These include

- Cisco Nonstop Forwarding (NSF)

- Stateful Switchover (SSO)

- Stackwise technology on 3750 switches

- Virtual Switch System (VSS)

- Monitoring tools such as SNMP and Syslog

- IP Service Level Agreement (SLA)

Each of these technologies is discussed in later sections of this chapter.

Some other technological features that enhance availability include server load balancing, firewall stateful failover, and fast routing convergence.

People

Although the "people" part of high availability is not usually under the control of the network engineer, it is an important part of the equation. The following items should be considered:

- **Staff work habits:** Staff should pay attention to detail, and their work should be reliable and consistent to make troubleshooting easier.

- **Staff skills and technical training:** A knowledgeable staff understands the network technologies and configures devices correctly. A company lab enables failover scenarios to be tested before incorporating them into the network and allows network engineers to practice their skills.

- **Communication and documentation:** There should be good communication between teams responsible for the network, security, servers, and applications. There should also be communication with users. Good documentation, readily available, is critical to understanding how the network is designed and how it should behave during a failure.

- **Sufficient time to accomplish a task:** Not having enough time to accomplish a network-related task leads to important components, such as testing and documentation, being left out. The design target should be a better than just "adequate" network.

- **Align staff with the services they support:** This helps ensure clear lines of responsibility for the different segments of the network. Be sure to include the people responsible for a segment in the planning for its high availability.

Processes

Companies that build repeatable processes and design templates have more cohesive networks and save time in troubleshooting problems. Process documentation should include configuration change procedures, failover and lab testing procedures, and network implementation procedures. These should be regularly reviewed and improved as part of the PPDIOO process.

A lab that reflects the current production network enables thorough testing and validation of such changes as new configurations and IOS versions and ensures that the staff thoroughly understands network failover processes.

Having a meaningful change control process includes the complete testing of all changes and how they affect failover within the entire network before they are implemented. Changes must be well planned with a roll-back strategy in place. A risk analysis can also help determine if the change is worthwhile.

Network management processes are often overlooked. These should include

- Capacity audits
- IOS version management
- Corporate best-practice design compliance
- Disaster recovery and business continuity plans
- Evaluating the security impact of a proposed change

Tools

A well-designed, highly available network can have a failure without it being noticed by users. It is important to have tools in place to monitor the network and send alerts when a failover occurs. Monitoring can also help spot problems as they begin to occur, enabling you to be proactive in your network management. There are many third-party tools available for this; some IOS tools are discussed in later sections of this chapter.

Good documentation is a critical tool to have. Good documentation includes up-to-date network diagrams with network addresses, VLAN information, and interface information. Important servers, applications, and services should be noted. Document not only HOW the network is designed, but also WHY it is designed that way.

Resiliency and High Availability

A highly available network is a resilient network. A resilient network employs various methods to allow it to recover and continue operating in the event of a failure. Resiliency leads to high availability through the following components:

- **Network-level resiliency (the focus of this book):** This includes redundant links and redundant devices, but it doesn't stop there. Those devices must be configured so they fail between devices, or links, quickly.

- **System-level resiliency:** This includes redundancy within the hardware, such as dual power supplies, and cold-standby parts, such as extra stackable switches or switch modules. It also includes features within the hardware that enable fast failover.

- **Network management and monitoring:** You need to detect a failure immediately and be informed of the actions taken automatically to remediate it.

Network Level Resiliency

Redundant links were discussed in Chapter 2. STP blocks a redundant link by default so that they are in an active/backup configuration. Etherchannels enables multiple links to be active. If a failure occurs they distribute traffic across the remaining links.

Configure your devices for fast convergence to avoid traffic drops when a link fails. RSTP is preferred over 802.1D STP because it provides faster failover. Use routing protocols such as EIGRP that have fast convergence times. You might need to tune the Layer 2 and Layer 3 protocol timers.

For accurate monitoring statistics, it is important that network clocks are synchronized. Use NTP for this. Syslog, SNMP, and IP SLA are some tools that help you monitor and track your network's resiliency. They are discussed in more detail in a future section.

Fast Failover

When measuring network resiliency, you must consider how long it takes for failover and convergence at all layers of the OSI stack, not just Layers 1–3. Table 5-1 outlines some of the typical convergence times.

Table 5-1   Convergence Times for Network Components

Network Component	Convergence Time
Rapid Spanning Tree	Subsecond for minor failures, 1–2 seconds for major failures.
Etherchannel	Approximately 1 second to redirect traffic to a different link in the channel.
First Hop Redundancy Protocols such as HSRP, VRRP, or GLBP	Default of 10 seconds. Recommended tuning of hello time to 1 second and hold time to 3 second yields a 3 second convergence time.
Routing Protocols	Subsecond for OSPF and EIGRP with recommended tuning of timers.
Switch Service Modules	Typically 3–5 seconds. Exception is Cisco Application Control Engine (ACE) with 1 second failover in active/active configuration.
Computer/Server TCP Stacks	9-second session teardown for Windows, longer for other OSs.

Optimizing Redundancy

You should be aware that redundancy does not always equal resiliency. Too much redundancy can increase the network complexity to a point that it becomes harder to troubleshoot and actually leads to a less-available network. There are too many paths for the data to follow, so it becomes less deterministic. The cost is much higher, also.

NSF with SSO

Layers 2–4 convergence time is enhanced in Cisco 4500 and 6500 series switches with redundant route processors (RP) by using NSF with SSO. When using this, only one RP is active. The standby RP synchronizes its configuration and dynamic state information (such as CEF, MAC, and FIB tables) with the active RP. When the active RP fails, SSO enables the standby RP to take over immediately. NSF keeps the switch forwarding traffic during the switchover, using the existing route and CEF tables. The goal of NSF with SSO is to prevent routing adjacencies from resetting, which prevents a routing flap. The switchover to the new RP must be completed before routing timers expire, or the router's neighbors will tear down their adjacency and routing will be disrupted.

When the new RP is up, the old routes are marked as stale, and the RP asks its routing peers to refresh them. When routing is converged, it updates the routing and CEF tables on the switch and the linecards.

NSF is supported with EIGRP, OSPF, ISIS, and BGP. An *NSF-capable router* supports NSF; an *NSF-aware router* does not support NSF but understands it and continues forwarding traffic during SSO.

Use NSF with SSO in locations where you do not have a duplicate switch for failover, such as at the user access or Enterprise network edge. Otherwise it can actually cause longer convergence. Routing protocols timers can be tuned very short to provide fast convergence. With SSO, the switchover to the standby RP might not occur before the tuned routing Dead timer expires, and the adjacency would be reset.

Designing for Redundancy

Figure 5-1 shows where you would typically use redundancy within a campus network. Access switches are either chassis-based with dual Supervisor engines and dual power supplies or are stackable switches. They have redundant, fully meshed links to redundant distribution switches, which, in turn, have redundant links to redundant core switches. Distribution and core switch pairs are connected via a Layer 2 or Layer 3 link. This design minimizes single points of failure and enables the network to recover from a link or switch failure.

Layer 2 Versus Layer 3 Access Design

You can use a Layer 2 or a Layer 3 access layer. When using L2, VLANs can either be distributed across multiple switches or local to each switch. Figure 5-2 shows L2 access switches with VLAN 10 on both of them. This design is not recommended. The FHRP Active switch and the STP Root must be statically configured as the same switch. STP blocks one uplink per access switch. RSTP helps speed convergence.

There must be a physical link between distribution switches, and it should be a L2 trunk. Without that link, any traffic between switches must go through an access switch. Additionally, failure of one of the access-to-distribution uplinks causes packets to be dropped until the FHRP dead timer expires.

Figure 5-1   Designing for Redundancy

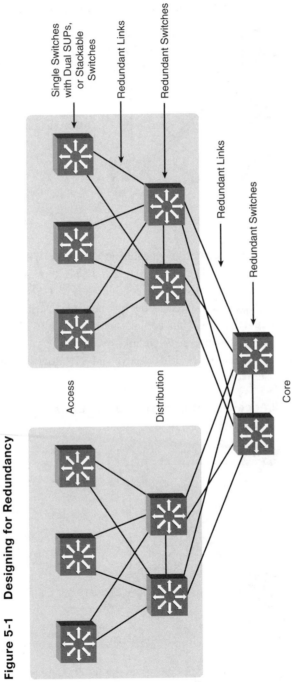

Figure 5-2   Layer 2 Access Switches with Distributed VLANs

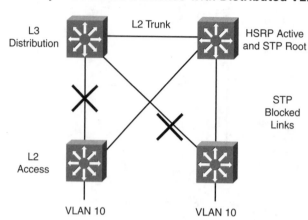

Figure 5-3 shows the recommended design when using L2 access switches. Each VLAN is local to one switch. The FHRP Active and STP Root must still be the same switch. They are still statically configured per VLAN so that traffic flow will be deterministic. Because the link between distribution switches is L3, there are no L2 loops. Thus no links are blocked by STP. However, traffic does not load balance between links because each switch forwards traffic only over the link to its HSRP Active and STP Root switch. RSTP is still used for faster convergence.

Figure 5-3   Layer 2 Access Switches with Local VLANs

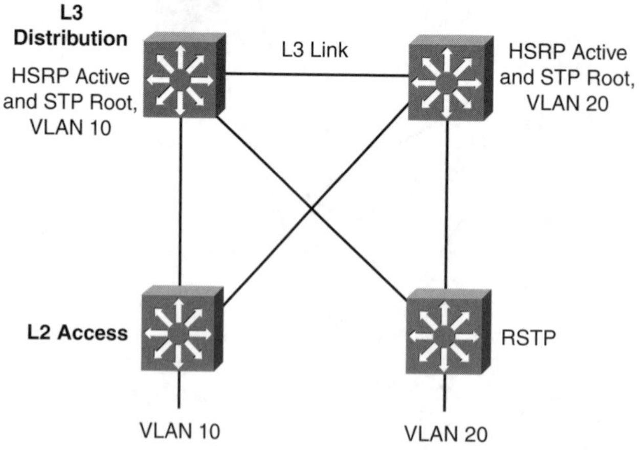

In Figure 5-4 the access switches are L3. This gives the faster convergence and is easiest to implement. All links between switches are L3. There is no need for HSRP, although STP should still be enabled in case of a misconfiguration. Access switches can load balance traffic across both uplinks. The access switches either run a routing protocol or use static routes. The distribution switches summarize routes for the access VLANs.

Figure 5-4   Layer 3 Access Switches

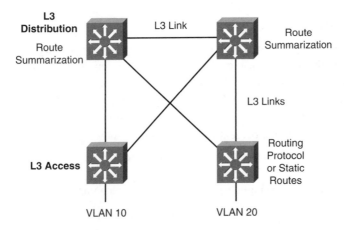

Using Nonchassis Based Access Switches

Using more than one stand-alone switch, such as the Cisco 3560 or 3750, in an access closet requires special design consideration. You can either daisy-chain the switches or use the Cisco Stackwise technology. When you daisy-chain switches, the top and bottom members of the chain typically uplink to one distribution switch each. You must add a link (or *loopback cable*) between the top and bottom switch. Otherwise, a failure in the link between two access switches might cause return traffic to be blackholed. Alternatively you can configure the link between the distribution switches as an L2 trunk.

Stackwise switches enable you to manage each group of access switches as one. Two stack member switches uplink to the distribution switches. Special cables connect the switches, and you should still connect the top and bottom members of the stack using a Stackwise cable. The link between distribution switches can then be an L3 link without worry of blackholing return traffic.

Network Management for High Availability

Network administrators use network management tools:

- To verify network performance

- To characterize, or baseline, network performance

- To understand amount and direction of traffic flow within the network

- To troubleshoot network problems

Syslog

Cisco devices produce system logging (or *syslog*) messages that can be output to the device console, VTY connection, system buffer, or remote syslog server. If sent to a syslog server, messages are sent on UDP port 514. You are probably familiar with the syslog message %SYS-5-CONFIG_I: Configured from console by console, for instance. A syslog message always starts with the percent sign and has the following format:

%FACILTY-SUBFACILITY-SEVERITY-MNEMONIC: message text

Each portion of a syslog message has a specific meaning:

- FACILITY-SUBFACILITY: This tells the protocol, module, or process that generated the message. Some examples are SYS for the operating system, OSPF, IF for an interface, and IP.

- SEVERITY: A number from 0 to 7 designating the importance of the action reported. The levels are

    - Emergency: 0

    - Alert: 1

    - Critical: 2

    - Error: 3

    - Warning: 4

    - Notice: 5

    - Informational: 6

    - Debugging: 7

- MNEMONIC: A code that identifies the action reported.

- A plain-text description of the event that triggered the syslog message.

SNMP

An SNMP manager collects information from SNMP agents residing on network devices, either through regular polling or by event-generated traps.

The information is stored on the local device in a Management Information Base (MIB). Access to the MIB is controlled by SNMP community strings. Access can be read-only (RO) or read-write(RW).

There are three versions of SNMP. Versions 1 and 2 send the community strings in clear text. They cannot authenticate the source of a message or encrypt a message. Therefore they should be used only for read-only access. SNMPv3 adds three security levels:

- `noAuthNoPriv`: Neither authenticates nor encrypts

- `authNoPriv`: Authenticates the sender but does not encrypt the message

- `authPriv`: Both authenticates the sender and encrypts the message

The following configuration creates a standard access list that allows only traffic sourced from the host at 10.1.1.1. Two community-strings are created, "ccnp" for read-only access and "c1sc0" for read-write access. Read-write access is permitted only from the host specified in access list 1. Next, the SNMP server address is given, along with the command to send traps messages to that server. Because SNMP version 3 is used, the username "admin" is needed:

```
sw1(config)# access-list 1 permit 10.1.1.1
sw1(config)# snmp-server community ccnp ro
sw1(config)# snmp-server community c1sc0 rw 1
sw1(config)# snmp-server host 10.1.1.2 traps admin
```

IP SLA

IP SLA is a feature that enables a Cisco router or switch to simulate specific types of traffic and send it to a receiver, called a *responder*. IP SLA probes can simulate various types of traffic, such as HTTP, FTP, DHCP, UDP jitter, UDP echo, HTTP, TCP connect, ICMP echo, ICMP path echo, ICMP path jitter, and DNS, and can report statistics such as path jitter. It has highly granular application configuration options such as TCP/UDP port numbers, TOS byte, and IP prefix bits. This is useful for measuring application performance end-to-end across your network. It can also be used to track reachability and then decrement HSRP priority values or bring up secondary links. Additionally, IP SLA can also be used as a measure of reliability and continuous availability. SNMP traps can be generated from events such as connection loss, timeout, roundtrip time threshold, average jitter threshold, one-way packet loss, one-way jitter, and one-way latency.

To enable IP SLA, configure the source to send the required type of data probes. The receiver can be a computer, or it can be another Cisco device. The configuration of a Cisco responder is simple. Use the global **ip sla responder** command. One benefit of using a Cisco device as the responder is that it can add time stamps to help measure latency and jitter. These time stamps take into account the device processing time so that the measurement reflects only network latency.

The configuration of the IP SLA source is more complex. You must create a monitor session, list the traffic type, responder IP address, and any other desired variables such as DSCP value. Then you schedule the probes. Optionally configure tracking using the IP SLA session. The following commands set up an IP SLA session that measures UDP jitter for a voice port. Traffic is sent every 120 seconds, starting when the last command is given and continues until it is manually stopped:

```
sw1(config)#ip sla 1
sw1(config-ip-sla)#udp-jitter 10.1.1.3 65422 codec g729a
sw1(config-ip-sla-jitter)#frequency 120
sw1(config-ip-sla-jitter)#exit
sw1(config)#ip sla schedule 1 life forever start-time now
```

## CHAPTER 6

First Hop Redundancy

Specifying a default gateway leads to a single point of failure. Proxy Address Resolution Protocol (ARP) is one method for hosts to dynamically discover gateways, but it has issues in a highly available environment. With Proxy ARP:

- Hosts ARP for all destinations, even remote.

- Router responds with its MAC.

- Problem: Slow failover because ARP entries take minutes to timeout.

Instead of making the host responsible for choosing a new gateway, router redundancy protocols enable two or more routers to support a shared MAC address. If the primary router is lost, the backup router assumes control of traffic forwarded to that MAC. This section refers to routers but includes those multilayer switches that can also implement Layer 3 redundancy.

Hot Standby Router Protocol

Hot Standby Router Protocol (HSRP) is a Cisco proprietary protocol.

With HSRP, two or more devices support a virtual router with a fictitious MAC address and unique IP address. Hosts use this IP address as their default gateway and the MAC address for the Layer 2 header. The virtual router's MAC address is 0000.0c07.AC*xx*, in which *xx* is the HSRP group. Multiple groups (virtual routers) are allowed.

The *Active* router forwards traffic. The *Standby* is backup. The standby monitors periodic hellos (multicast to 224.0.0.2, UDP port 1985) to detect a failure of the active router. On failure, the standby device starts answering messages sent to the IP and MAC addresses of the virtual router.

The active router is chosen because it has the highest HSRP priority (default priority is 100). In case of a tie, the router with the highest configured IP address wins the election. A new router with a higher priority does not cause an election unless it is configured to *preempt*—that is, take over from a lower priority router. Configuring a router to preempt also ensures that the highest priority router regains its active status if it goes down but then comes back online again.

Interface tracking reduces the active router's priority if a specified circuit is down. This enables the standby router to take over even though the active router is still up.

HSRP States

HSRP devices move between these states:

- **Initial:** HSRP is not running.

- **Learn:** The router does not know the virtual IP address and is waiting to hear from the active router.

- **Listen:** The router knows the IP and MAC of the virtual router, but it is not the active or standby router.

- **Speak:** Router sends periodic HSRP hellos and participates in the election of the active router.

- **Standby:** Router monitors hellos from active router and assumes responsibility if active router fails.

- **Active:** Router forwards packets on behalf of the virtual router.

Note

The Learn state is not actually seen in debugs of HSRP.

Configuring HSRP

To begin configuring HSRP, use the **standby** *group-number* **ip** *virtual-IP-address* command in interface configuration mode. Routers in the same HSRP group must belong to the same subnet/virtual LAN (VLAN.) Give this command under the interface connecting to that subnet or VLAN. For instance, use the following to configure the router as a member of HSRP group 39 with virtual router IP address 10.0.0.1:

```
Router(config-if)# standby 39 ip 10.0.0.1
```

HSRP authentication helps prevent unauthorized routers from seeing user traffic:

```
Router(config-if)# stand 2 authentication md5 key-string cisco
```

Tune HSRP with four options: Priority, Preempt, Timers, and Interface Tracking.

Manually select the active router by configuring its priority higher than the default of 100:

```
Router(config-if)# standby 39 priority 150
```

Along with configuring priority, configure **preempt** to enable a router to take over if the active router has lower priority, as shown in the following commands. This helps lead to a predictable data path through the network. The second command shown delays preemption until the router or switch has fully booted and the routing protocol has converged. Time how long it takes to boot and add 50 percent to get the delay value in seconds:

```
Router(config-if)# standby 39 preempt
Router(config-if)# standby 39 preempt delay minimum 90
```

Speed convergence by changing the hello and hold times. The following sets the hello interval to 1 second and the hold time to 3 seconds. They can be set between 1–255 seconds (the default hello is 3 seconds and hold time is 10 seconds):

```
Router(config-if)# standby 39 timers 1 3
```

Tracking an interface can trigger an election if the active router is still up but a critical interface (such as the one to the Internet) is down. In the following, if serial 1/0/0 is down, the router's HSRP priority is decremented by 100 (the default value to decrement is 10):

```
Router(config-if)# standby 39 track s1/0/0 100
```

Another way to track an indirect connection is to use IP SLA (described in Chapter 5). With IP SLA tracking, HSRP can failover to the standby router if any connection on the path to a remote location fails or exceeds link-quality thresholds. The following sample configuration shows how to add tracking an IP SLA session number 5 to an existing HSRP interface configuration:

```
Router(config)#ip sla 5
Router(config-ip-sla)# udp-jitter 172.17.1.2 16000
Router(config)#track 10 rtr 5
Router(config-if)# int fa 1/0/15
Router(config-if)# stand 2 track 10 decrement 50
```

Note

The standby router must be configured with the preempt command for it to take control.

Multiple HSRP standby groups can be configured, and the same router can be active for some groups and standby for others by adjusting priorities. You

can have a maximum of 255 groups. When using Layer 3 switches, configure the same switch as the primary HSRP router and the Spanning Tree root.

Virtual Router Redundancy Protocol

Virtual Router Redundancy Protocol (VRRP) is similar to HSRP, but it is an
open standard (RFC 2338). Two or more devices act as a virtual router. With
VRRP, however, the IP address used can be either a virtual one or the actual
IP address of the primary router. VRRP is supported only on Cisco 4500 and
6500 series switches.

The VRRP *Master* router forwards traffic. The master is chosen because it
owns the real address, or it has the highest priority. (The default is 100.) If a
real address is supported, the owner of real address *must* be master. A
Backup router takes over if the master fails, and there can be multiple
backup routers. They monitor periodic hellos multicast by the master to
224.0.0.18, using UDP port 112, to detect a failure of the master router.

Multiple VRRP groups are allowed, just as with HSRP.

Routers in the same VRRP group must belong to the same subnet/VLAN. To
enable VRRP, give this command **vrrp** *group-number* **ip** *virtual-IP-address*
under the interface connecting to that subnet or VLAN:

```
Router(config-if) # vrrp 39 ip 10.0.0.1
```

Control the master and backup elections by configuring priority values from
1–255. If a master VRRP router is shut down, it advertises a priority of 0.
This triggers the backup routers to hold an election without waiting for the
master's hellos to time out.

```
Router(config-if)# vrrp 39 priority 175
```

VRRP uses the following timers:

- Advertisement, or hello, interval in seconds. Default is 1 second.

- Master down interval. Equals 3 x advertisement interval plus skew
  time. Similar to a hold or dead timer.

- Skew time. (256–priority) / 256. This is meant to ensure that the
  highest priority backup router becomes master because higher priority
  routers have shorter master down intervals.

To change the timers on the master, use the following command because it is
the router that advertises the hellos:

```
Router(config-if)# vrrp 39 timers advertise 5
```

To change the timers on the backup routers, use the following command because they hear the hellos from the master:

```
Router(config-if)# vrrp 39 timers learn
```

VRRP cannot track interfaces but can track IP SLA object groups.

GLBP

One issue with both HSRP and VRRP is that only the primary router is in use; the others must wait for the primary to fail before they are used. These two protocols use groups to get around that limitation. However, Gateway Load Balancing Protocol (GLBP) enables the simultaneous use of up to four gateways, thus maximizing bandwidth. With GLBP, there is still one virtual IP address. However, each participating router has a virtual MAC address, and different routers' virtual MAC addresses are sent in answer to ARPs for the virtual IP address. GLBP can also use groups up to a maximum of 1024 per physical interface. GLBP is supported only on Cisco 4500 and 6500 series switches.

The load sharing is done in one of three ways:

- **Weighted load balancing:** Traffic is balanced proportional to a configured weight.

- **Host-dependent load balancing:** A given host always uses the same router.

- **Round-robin load balancing:** Each router MAC is used to respond to ARP requests in turn.

GLBP routers elect an Active Virtual Gateway (AVG). It is the only router to respond to ARPs. It uses this capacity to balance the load among the GLBP routers. The highest priority router is the AVG; the highest configured IP address is used in case of a tie.

The actual router used by a host is its Active Virtual Forwarder (AVF). GLBP group members multicast hellos every 3 seconds to IP address 224.0.0.102, UDP port 3222. If one router goes down, another router answers for its MAC address.

Configure GLBP with the interface command **glbp** *group-number* **ip** *virtual-IP-address,* as shown:

```
Router(config-if)# glbp 39 ip 10.0.0.1
```

To ensure deterministic elections, each router can be configured with a priority. The default priority is 100:

```
Router(config-if)# glbp 39 priority 150
```

Hello and hold (or dead) timers can be configured for each interface with the command **glbp** *group-number* **timers [msec]** *hello-time* **[msec]** *hold-time*. Values are in seconds unless the **msec** keyword is used.

GLBP can also track interfaces just as with HSRP. If a tracked interface goes down, another router answers for the first router's MAC address.

Planning Router Redundancy Implementation

Before configuring first-hop redundancy, determine which protocol is best in your network. If you have the same VLAN on multiple access switches, use HSRP or VRRP. If you use local VLANs, contained to a single switch, GLBP is an option.

Before configuring HSRP or VRRP on a multilayer switch, determine which switch is the root bridge for each VLAN. The root bridge should be the active HSRP/VRRP router. Determine priorities to be used, and whether you need tracking or timer adjustment.

After your implementation, verify and test. To view the switch's standby status, use the **show standby interface** *interface* command or **show standby brief**. To monitor standby activity, use the **debug standby** command.

CHAPTER 7

Campus Network Security

Attention has traditionally been paid to network perimeter security, such as firewall, and to mitigating Layer 3 attacks. However, networks must be protected against Layer 2 attacks, too. These are launched from devices inside the network by either a rogue device or a legitimate device that has been compromised. Rogue devices might be placed maliciously or might just be connected to an access switch by an employee wanting more switch port or wireless access. They include

- Wireless routers or hubs

- Access switches

- Hubs

A switch might become the Spanning Tree root bridge and disrupt user traffic. Use **root guard** and **bpdu guard** commands to prevent this. (Spanning Tree security is discussed later in this chapter.)

The following are four typical types of attacks against a switched network:

- **MAC address-based attacks:** MAC address flooding

- **VLAN-based attacks:** VLAN hopping and attacks against devices on the same VLAN

- **Spoofing attacks:** DHCP spoofing, MAC spoofing, Address Resolution Protocol (ARP) spoofing, and Spanning Tree attacks

- **Attacks against the switch:** Cisco Discovery Protocol (CDP) manipulation, Telnet attacks, and Secure Shell (SSH) attacks

MAC Address-Based Attacks

Common MAC address-based attacks rely on flooding the CAM table and can be mitigated by using port security and port-based authentication.

MAC Address Flooding

In a MAC address flooding attack, the attacker fills the switch's Content Addressable Memory (CAM) table with invalid MAC addresses. After the table is full, all traffic with an address not in the table is flooded out all interfaces. This has two bad effects: more traffic on the LAN and more work for the switch. This can also cause the CAM tables of adjacent switches to overflow. Additionally, the intruder's traffic is also flooded, so they have access to more ports than they would normally have. After the attack stops, CAM entries age out and life returns to normal. However, meanwhile the attacker might have captured a significant amount of data.

Port security and port-based authentication can help mitigate MAC address attacks.

Port Security

Port security limits the number of MAC addresses allowed per port and can also limit which MAC addresses are allowed. Allowed MAC addressed can be manually configured or the switch can sticky learn them. Table 8-1 lists port security commands; these are given at the interface.

Table 7-1 Port Security Commands

Command	Description
`switchport port-security`	Enables port security on that interface.
`switchport port-security maximum value`	Specifies the max MAC addresses allowed on this port. Default is 1.
`switchport port-security violation {shutdown | restrict | protect}`	Configures the action to be taken when the maximum number is reached and a MAC address not associated with the port attempts to use the port, or when a station whose MAC address is associated with a different port attempt to access this port. Default is shutdown.
`switchport port-security mac-address mac-address`	Statically associates a specific MAC address with a port.
`switchport port-security mac-address sticky`	Enables the switch port to dynamically learn secure MAC addresses. MAC addresses learned through that port, up to the maximum number, if a maximum is configured, are treated as secure MAC addresses.
`show port security [interface interface | address]`	Verifies port security actions.

The following commands show how to verify the port security configuration:

```
Switch# show port-security interface fa 1/0/15
Port Security              : Enabled
Port Status                : Secure-Up
Violation Mode             : Shutdown
Aging Time                 : 0 mins
Aging Type                 : Absolute
SecureStatic Address Aging : Disabled
Maximum MAC Addresses      : 2
Total MAC Addresses        : 0
Configured MAC Addresses   : 0
Sticky MAC Addresses       : 0
Last Source Address:Vlan   : 0000.0000.0000:0
Security Violation Count   : 0
```

Port-Based Authentication

802.1x authentication requires a computer (called a client) to be authenticated before it is allowed access to the LAN. This can be combined with port security to enable only authenticated clients with specified MAC addresses to access a port. When a computer connects to a switch port configured for 802.1x authentication, it follows these steps:

Step 1. The port is in the *unauthorized* state, allowing only 802.1x EAP over LAN (EAPOL) traffic.

Step 2. The client connects to the port. The switch either requests authentication or the client sends an EAPOL frame to begin authentication.

Step 3. The switch relays authentication information between the client and a RADIUS server that acts in proxy for the client.

Step 4. If authentication succeeds, the port transitions to the *authorized* state, and normal LAN traffic is allowed through it.

Table 7-2 shows commands to configure 802.1x authentication on a switch.

Table 7-2   Configuring 802.1x Port Authentication

Command	Description
`(config)#aaa new-model`	Enables AAA on the switch
`(config)#aaa authentication dot1x default group radius`	Creates a AAA method list that says to use 802.1x authentication by default, using a RADIUS server (configured separately)
`(config)#dot1x system-auth-control`	Globally enables 802.1x authentication on the switch
`(config-if)#dot1x port-control [auto | force-authorized | force-unauthorized]`	Enables 802.1x authentication on an interface of the switch and sets default port state
`show dot1x`	Verifies 802.1x authentication

VLAN-Based Attacks

VLAN-based attacks include VLAN hopping, in which a station can access a VLAN other than its own. This can be done with switch spoofing or with 802.1Q double-tagging.

Switch Spoofing

Switch spoofing involves a station configured to negotiate a trunk link between itself and the switch. By default, switches dynamically negotiate trunking status using Dynamic Trunking Protocol (DTP). If a computer can use DTP to establish a trunk link to the switch, it receives all traffic bound for every VLAN allowed on that trunk. By default, all VLANs are allowed on a trunk.

You can mitigate this by turning off DTP on all ports that should not become trunks, such as most access ports, using the interface command **switchport nonegotiate**. If the port should be an access port, configure it as such with the interface command **switchport mode access** and turn off CDP on that port. Additionally, shut down all unused ports and assign them to an unused VLAN. The commands to do this are

```
Switch(config)# interface interface
Switch(config-if)# switchport mode access
Switch(config-if)# switchport access vlan vlan
Switch(config-if)# shutdown
```

802.1Q Double-Tagging

A double-tagging attack is possible because 802.1Q trunking does not tag
frames from the native VLAN. In this attack, the attacking computer negotiates a trunk port between itself and the switch and then generates frames
with two 802.1Q tags. The first tag matches the native VLAN of the trunk
port, and the second matches the VLAN of a host it wants to attack, as
shown in Figure 7-1. The first switch in the path strips off the first 802.1Q
tag and forwards it to adjacent switches. The next switch forwards the frame
based on the VLAN listed in the second tag.

The double-tagging method of a VLAN hopping attack works even if trunk
ports are set to off, if the trunk has the same VLAN as the attacker.

Figure 7-1   VLAN Hopping by 802.1Q Double-Tagging

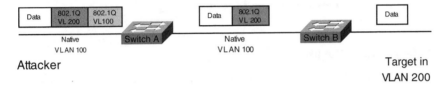

Switch A removes the first tag for VLAN 100 because it matches the native
VLAN for that link. It forwards the frame out all links with the same native
VLAN, including its link to Switch B. Switch B sees the frame come in with
an 802.1Q tag for VLAN 200, so it forwards it out the VLAN 200 link to the
victim computer.

To mitigate this type of attack, use the same strategies used for switch spoofing. You can also use VLAN access control lists, called *VACLs*, or implement
Private VLANs.

VACLs

Cisco switches support of various kinds of ACLs:

- Traditional Router ACL (RACL)

- QoS ACL

- VACL

VLAN access control lists (VACL) are similar to route-maps because they
are composed of statements that contain match and set conditions. In a
VACL, the "set" conditions are called "actions." Actions include **forward**,
drop, and **redirect**. Like route-maps, VACL statements are numbered for

ordering. After configuration, VACLs are applied to traffic to specified VLANs.

The following is a sample VACL that instructs the switch to drop traffic matching ACL 101 (not shown) and forward all other traffic:

```
Switch(config)# vlan access-map Drop101 10
Switch(config-access-map)# match ip address 101
Switch(config-access-map)# action drop
!
Switch(config-access-map)# vlan access-map Drop101 20
Switch(config-access-map)# action forward
!
Switch(config)# vlan filter Drop101 vlan-list 10
```

To view VACL settings, use the commands **show vlan access-map** *vacl_name* or **show vlan filter access-map** *vacl_name*.

Private VLANs

Private VLANs (PVLAN) enable large companies or service providers to isolate users into separate multiaccess domains. Using a VLAN for each group is not scalable. For instance, the switch's maximum VLANs would limit the number of customers an ISP can have. Each VLAN requires a separate IP subnet, which could also be a limiting factor.

PVLANs divide a VLAN into secondary VLANs, letting you isolate a set of ports from other ports within the same VLAN. There are two types of secondary VLANs:

- **Community VLANs:** Ports can communicate with other ports in the same community VLAN.
- **Isolated VLANs:** Ports cannot communicate with each other.

Ports within a private VLAN can be one of three types:

- **Community:** Communicates with other community ports and with promiscuous ports
- **Isolated:** Communicates only with promiscuous ports
- **Promiscuous:** Communicates with all ports

Table 7-3 shows the commands to configure a primary private VLAN, secondary PVLANs, and their associated ports.

Table 7-3   Configuring Private VLANs

Command	Description
`vlan vlan-id`	Enters VLAN configuration mode.
`private-vlan {community | isolated | primary}`	Configures the VLAN as a private VLAN and specifies the type. Repeat this command to configure all primary and secondary VLANs
`vlan primary-vlan-id`	Enters configuration mode for the primary VLAN.
`private-vlan association secondary_vlan_list`	Associates secondary VLANs with the primary one. Separate the secondary VLAN numbers with a comma, no spaces.
`switchport mode private-vlan {host |promiscuous}`	Configures a port as either a host port (for community or isolated) or a promiscuous port.
`switchport private-vlan host-association primary_vlan_ ID secondary_vlan_ID`	Associates a host port with its primary and secondary PVLANs
`private-vlan mapping primary_ vlan_ID secondary_vlan_list`	Associates a promiscuous port with its primary and secondary PVLANs.
`show interfaces interface switchport`	Verifies the VLAN configuration.
`show interfaces private-vlan mapping`	Verify the private VLAN configuration.

Protected Ports

On some lower-end switches, protected ports can provide a simple version of private VLANs. Traffic from a protected port can access only an unprotected port. Traffic between protected ports is blocked. Configure port protection at the interface:

```
Switch(config-if)# port protected
```

Spoof Attacks

Spoof attacks include DHCP spoofing, MAC address spoofing, and ARP spoofing.

DHCP Spoofing

A DHCP spoofing attacker listens for DHCP requests and answers them, giving its IP address as the client default gateway. The attacker then becomes a "man-in-the-middle" as all off-net traffic flows through it.

DHCP snooping can prevent DHCP spoofing attacks. When DHCP snooping is enabled, only ports that uplink to an authorized DHCP server are trusted and allowed to send all types of DHCP messages. All other ports on the switch are untrusted and can send only DHCP requests. If a DHCP response (or "offer") is seen on an untrusted port, the port is shut down. The switch can also be configured to send information, such as port ID, using DHCP option 82.

Note

DHCP snooping configuration is user impacting because the switch drops all DHCP requests until the ports are configured. You should do this during off hours or during a maintenance window.

Configure DHCP snooping with the following commands, either globally or for a particular VLAN. Configure only individual ports that uplink to DHCP servers as trusted ports.

```
Switch(config)# ip dhcp snooping
Switch(config)# ip dhcp snooping information option
Switch(config)# ip dhcp snooping vlan number number
Switch(config-if)# ip dhcp snooping trust
Switch(config-if)# ip dhcp snooping limit pkts-per-second
Switch# show ip dhcp snooping
```

IP Source Guard

To extend the protection further, IP Source Guard tracks the IP addresses of the host connected to each port and prevents traffic sourced from another IP address from entering that port. The tracking can be done based on just an IP address or on both IP and MAC addresses.

Enable IP Source Guard for both IP and MAC addresses on host access interfaces with the command **ip verify source port-security**.

ARP Spoofing

In an ARP spoofing attack, the attacker sends out gratuitous (unsolicited) ARP messages giving the IP address of the local default gateway, with its own MAC address as the Layer 2 address. Local devices overwrite their existing correct ARP information with the incorrect one, and, thus, they forward off-net traffic to the attacker (it becomes a "man-in-the-middle"). If the attacker then forwards it on to the legitimate router, this type of attack might go undetected by the users.

Dynamic ARP Inspection (DAI) can work with DHCP spoofing to stop ARP spoofing. DAI defines trusted and untrusted interfaces. It intercepts ARP messages on untrusted ports and checks them against the IP address/MAC address bindings in the DHCP snooping database. They must match for the switch to forward the traffic. Access ports should be configured as untrusted, and ports that connect to other switches or to a router should be trusted.

Enable DAI on a VLAN, or multiple VLANs, and configure trusted interfaces. You can optionally configure a rate limit or configure which addresses DAI matches against. (The default is IP and MAC address.) The basic commands are

```
Switch(config)# ip arp inspection vlan vlan_id
Switch(config-if)# ip arp inspection trust
```

Securing Your Switch

Here are some basic security suggestions for network devices:

- Use passwords that are not susceptible to a dictionary attack. Add numbers or substitute numbers and symbols for letters.

- Limit Telnet access using access lists.

- Use SSH instead of Telnet.

- Physically secure access to the device.

- Use banners that warn against unauthorized access.

- Remove unused services, such as finger, the TCP and UDP small servers, service config, and HTTP server.

- Set up and monitor Syslog.

- Disable automatic trunking on all nontrunk ports.

- Disable CDP on ports where it is not needed.

## CHAPTER 8

Voice and Video in a Campus Network

Voice over IP (VoIP) has become common in the business world, and now Video over IP is becoming more integrated into networks. Neither should be added to a network without advance planning to ensure good voice and video quality. Some benefits of converging voice, video, and data networks include

- **Consolidating network expenses:** Only one wire and one switch port are needed per user. One network to provision and manage.

- **More efficient bandwidth use:** Bandwidth can be used for data when there is not an active voice/video session.

- **Lower telephony costs:** Internal calls use the data network, rather than the PSTN.

- **Innovative services:** Ability to unify a company's various methods of communication.

- **For service providers, the ability to sell new services:** Can lead to increased revenue, flexibility in pricing, and access to new communication devices.

Voice, video, and data have different network requirements. Voice requirements include low bandwidth, little delay, small amounts of jitter (variable delay), small amounts of packet loss, a highly available network, and PoE. Security requirements are about average, but management is highly important.

Video requirements depend on whether it is a one-way stream or an interactive video session. One-way streams use a fairly steady amount of bandwidth but in interactive sessions the bandwidth varies widely. Typical requirements include high bandwidth, little delay, small amounts of jitter, and little packet loss. High availability is not as important, and PoE is not needed. Security and management needs are medium.

Data requirements typically include high bandwidth, but delay and jitter are not crucial. A highly available network is needed, but PoE is not. Data security should be high, with medium management levels.

VoIP in a Campus Network

Figure 8-1 shows some components of a VoIP system, which can include the following:

- **IP phones:** Provide voice and applications to the user

- **Cisco Unified Communications Manager (UCM):** Serves as an IP PBX. Registers phones, controls calls

- **Voice gateways:** Translates between PSTN and IP calls and provides backup to the Cisco UCM (IP PBX, or Call Agent)

- **Gatekeepers:** An optional component that can do call admission control, allocate bandwidth for calls, and resolve phone numbers into IP addresses

- **Video conferencing unit:** Allows voice and video in the same phone call

- **Multipoint control unit:** Allows multiple participants to join an audio or video conference call

- **Application server:** Provides services such as Unity voice mail and Presence

Figure 8-1   Some Components of a VoIP System

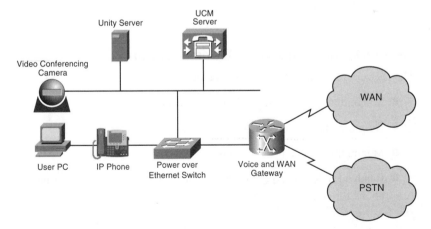

VoIP traffic consists of two types: voice bearer and call control signaling. Voice bearer traffic is carried over the UDP-based Real Time Protocol (RTP). Call control uses one of several different protocols to communicate between the phone and UCM and between the UCM and the voice gateways.

Preparing the Network for VoIP

When adding voice or video to an existing network, you should examine several things in advance to provide the high level of availability users expect in their phone system:

- **What features are needed?:** Power for IP phones, security for voice calls, and Quality of Service (QoS) to control bandwidth, delay, jitter, and packet loss.

- **The physical plant:** Cabling at least CAT-5.

- **Electrical power for the IP phones:** Use either PoE from Catalyst switch or power inline module, or a power brick.

- **Bandwidth:** Commit no more than 75 percent of bandwidth. Consider all types of traffic: voice, video, and data. Have more than enough bandwidth if possible. Include both voice and call-control traffic in your planning.

- **Network management:** Monitor and proactively manage the network so that it is always available. Need voice VLANs on the switches and DHCP for the phones.

- **High availability:** Provide redundant hardware and links. Need uninterruptible power supply (UPS) with auto-restart, monitoring, and four-hour response contract. Might need generator backup. Maintain correct operating temperatures.

Network and Bandwidth Considerations

The network requirements for VoIP include:

- Maximum delay of 150–200 ms (one-way)

- No more than 1 percent packet loss

- Maximum average jitter of 30 ms

- Bandwidth of 21–106 kbps per call, plus approximately 150 bps per phone for control traffic

A formula to use when calculating bandwidth needed for voice calls is as follows:

(Packet payload + all headers) × Packet rate per second

Voice VLANs

Cisco switches can be configured to dynamically place IP telephones into a Voice, or auxiliary, VLAN separate from the data VLANs. They can do this even when the phone and PC are physically connected to the same switch port. Voice VLANs enable phones to be dynamically placed in a separate IP subnet from hosts, to have QoS (using 802.1Q/p headers) and security policies applied, and make troubleshooting easier.

Cisco IP phones have a small internal switch that places an 802.1q tag on voice traffic and marks the Class of Service (CoS) bits in the tag. Data traffic is sent untagged over the native VLAN. The switch port does not actually become a trunk and still can be configured as an access port. It is considered a multi-VLAN access port.

Power over Ethernet (PoE) Switches

IP phones can receive power from PoE switches, eliminating the need for an electrical plug.

Two power standards are the Cisco Inline PoE and the IEEE's 802.3af standard. Both have a method for sensing that a powered device is connected to the port. 802.3af specifies a method for determining the amount of power needed by the device. Cisco devices, when connected to Cisco switches, can additionally use CDP to send that information. Most IP phones require no more than 15 W of power specified in 802.3af, but some new phones, access points, and surveillance cameras require more. The 802.3at standard will specify up to 30 W of power. Some Cisco switches can currently supply up to 20 W.

Because a switch assumes 15.4 W of power until the connected device tells it the amount needed (via CDP), calculate your power budget based on 15.4 W for all devices because if the switch reboots, all ports will ask for 15.4 W until they get the correct information. Non-CDP devices always get allocated 15.4 W.

Cisco PoE switches automatically detect and provide power. To disable this function, or to reenable it, use the interface command **power inline {never | auto}**. To view interfaces and the power allotted to each, use **show power inline** [*interface*].

QoS for VoIP

QoS gives special treatment to certain traffic at the expense of others. Using QoS in the network has several advantages:

- Prioritizes access to resources so that critical traffic can be served

- Allows good management of network resources

- Allows service to be tailored to network needs

- Allows mission-critical applications to share the network with other data

People sometimes think that there is no need for QoS strategies in a LAN. However, switch ports can experience congestion because of port speed mismatches, many people trying to access the switch backbone, and many people trying to send traffic to the same switch port (such as a server port). Voice and video traffic contends with, and can be affected by, data traffic within both the WAN and the LAN.

QoS Actions

Three QoS strategies are commonly implemented on interfaces in which traffic enters the switch:

- **Classification:** Distinguishing one type of traffic from another. After traffic is classified, other actions can be performed on it. Some classification methods include access lists, ingress interface, and NBAR.

- **Marking:** At Layer 2, placing an 802.1p CoS value within the 802.1Q frame tag. At Layer 3, setting IP Precedence or Differentiated Services Code Point (DSCP) values in the packet's IP header.

- **Policing:** Determining whether a specific type of traffic is within preset bandwidth levels. If so, it is usually allowed and might be marked. If not, the traffic is typically marked or dropped. CAR and class-based policing are examples of policing techniques.

Other QoS techniques are typically used on outbound interfaces:

- **Traffic shaping and conditioning:** Attempts to send traffic out in a steady stream at a specified rate. Buffers traffic that goes above that rate and sends it when there is less traffic on the line.

- **Queuing:** After traffic is classified and marked, one way it can be given special treatment is to be put into different queues on the interface to be sent out at different rates and times. Some examples include priority queuing, weighted fair queuing, and custom queuing. The default queuing method for a switch port is FIFO.

- **Dropping:** Normall interface queues accept packets until they are full and then drop everything after that. You can implement prioritized dropping so that less important packets are dropped before more important ones, such as with Weighted Random Early Detection (WRED).

DSCP Values

Differentiated services provide levels of service based on the value of certain bits in the IP header or the 802.1Q tag. Each hop along the way must be configured to treat the marked traffic the way you want; this is called per-hop behavior (PHB).

In the Layer 2 802.1q tag, you use the three 802.1p bits to set the CoS value. Voice is usually set to 5 and video to 4.

In the Layer 3 IP header, you use the 8-bit ToS field. You can set either IP Precedence using the top 3 bits or Differentiated Services Code Points (DSCP) using the top 6 bits of the field. The bottom 2 bits are set aside for congestion notification. The default DSCP value is 0, which corresponds to best-effort delivery.

The six DSCP bits can be broken down into two sections: The first 3 bits define the DiffServ Assured Forwarding (AF) class, and the next 2 bits define the drop probability within that class. The sixth bit is 0 and unused. AF classes 1–4 are defined, and within each class, 1 is low drop probability, 2 is medium, and 3 is high (meaning that traffic is more likely to get dropped if there is congestion). These are shown in Table 8-1.

Table 8-1   DSCP Assured Forwarding Values

	Low Drop	Medium Drop	High Drop
Class 1	AF11	AF12	AF13
Class 2	AF21	AF22	AF23
Class 3	AF31	AF32	AF33
Class 4	AF41	AF42	AF43

Voice bearer traffic uses an Expedited Forwarding value of DSCP 46 to give it higher priority within the network.

Trust Boundaries

When IP traffic comes in already marked, the switch has some options about how to handle it. It can

- Trust the DSCP value in the incoming packet, if present.

- Trust the IP Precedence value in the incoming packet, if present.

- Trust the CoS value in the incoming frame, if present.

- Classify the traffic based on an IP access control list or a MAC address access control list.

Mark traffic for QoS as close to the source as possible. If the source is an IP telephone, it can mark its own traffic. If not, the building access module switch can do the marking. If those are not under your control, you might need to mark at the distribution layer. Classifying and marking slows traffic flow, so do not do it at the core. All devices along the path should then be configured to trust the marking and provide a level of service based on it. The place where trusted marking is done is called the trust boundary.

Configuring VoIP Support on a Switch

Before implementing VoIP, plan the following:

1. **PoE:** Ensure that enough power is available for all phones, with a UPS backup.

2. **Voice VLAN:** Determine the number of VLANs needed and the associated IP subnets. Add DHCP scopes for the phones, and add the phone networks to the routing protocol.

3. **QoS:** Decide which marking and queues will be used. Implement AutoQoS and then tune as needed.

4. **Fast Convergency:** To enhance high availability, tune the routing and HSRP/VRRP/GLBP timers.

5. **Test Plan:** Test the voice implementation thoroughly before converting users to it. Check that both the phone and PC get the correct IP addresses, that the phone registers with the UCM, and that calls to and from the phone succeed.

Manual Configuration

To associate a voice VLAN with a switch port, use the following:

```
Switch(config-if)# switchport voice vlan vlan-ID
```

To configure an IOS switch to trust the markings on traffic entering an interface, use the following:

```
Switch(config-if)# mls qos trust {dscp | cos}
```

To configure the switch to trust the traffic markings only if a Cisco phone is connected, use the following:

```
Switch(config-if)# mls qos trust device cisco-phone
```

To set a COS value for frames coming from a PC attached to the phone, use the following:

```
Switch(config-if)# switchport priority extend cos cos-value
```

To verify the interface parameters, use the following:

```
Switch(config-if)# show interfaces interface switchport
```

To verify the QoS parameters on an interface, use the following:

```
Switch(config-if)# show mls qos interface interface
```

Using AutoQoS

When AutoQoS is enabled, the switch configures its interfaces based on a best-practices template. AutoQoS has the following benefits:

- Automatic discovery and classification of network applications.

- Creates QoS policies for those applications.

- Configures the switch to support Cisco IP phones and network applications. Manual configuration can also be done afterward.

- Sets up SNMP traps for network reporting.

- Configures consistently across your network when used on all routers and switches.

CDP must be enabled for AutoQoS to function properly with Cisco IP phones.

AutoQoS commands for switches running Native IOS are shown in Table 8-3.

Table 8-3   AutoQoS Commands for IOS

Command	Description
(config-if)#**auto qos voip trust**	Configures the port to trust the COS on all traffic entering the port.
(config-if)#**auto qos voip cisco-phone**	Configures the port to trust traffic markings only if a Cisco phone is connected to the port. Requires that CDP be enabled.
#**show auto qos [interface** *interface*]	Shows the AutoQoS configuration. Does not show any manual QoS configuration: Use **show run** to see that.

Video over IP

Video traffic roughly falls into one of three categories: many-to-many, many-to-few, and few-to-many.

Many-to-many includes interactive video, such as Telepresence, Webex, desktop video conferencing, and other peer-to-peer video and collaboration applications. The data flow is client-to-client, or MCU-to-client. Bandwidth needs for high definition video vary during the session but are high-up to 12 Mb/s per location, with compression.

Many-to-few sessions represent IP surveillance cameras. The video flow is from the camera source to a storage location, from storage to a client, or from the source to a client. These typically require up to 4 Mb/s of bandwidth per camera.

Few-to-many describes the typical streaming video, either from an internal company source or an Internet source. It also applies to digital signage media. This is the most predictable of all video streams and users typically tolerate less-than-perfect quality. Traffic flows are from storage-to-client or from server-to-client.

QoS Requirements for Video

Video traffic should be compressed because of its high bandwidth needs, but this causes a lot of variation in network traffic. A picture that does not change much can compress well, resulting in fairly low bandwidth use. But when there are a lot of changes in the picture, such as when someone moves or shares a new document, compression does not work as well, which results in high bandwidth use. In contrast, voice traffic is fairly steady.

Video should be placed in its own queue and might be prioritized depending on company requirements. Consider placing interactive and streaming video into different queues. Aim to provide no more than 200 ms of latency for most video applications.

Make sure that there is sufficient bandwidth in the network before adding video applications.

## CHAPTER 9

Wireless LANs in a Campus Network

Wireless LANs (WLAN) transmit and receive data using radio or infrared signals, sent through an access point (AP), and are not usually required to have radio frequency (RF) licenses. WLANs are local to a building or a campus and are an extension of the wired network.

Cisco Unified Wireless Network

The Cisco Unified Wireless Network concept has five components that work together to create a complete network, from client devices to network infrastructure, to network applications. Cisco has equipment appropriate to each component. Table 9-1 lists components and equipment.

Table 9-1   Cisco Unified Wireless Network Components

Component	Description and Device
Client devices	Cisco client and Cisco compatible third-party vendor clients
Mobility platform	APs and bridges using LWAPP
Network unification	Leverages existing wired network. Includes WLAN controllers and switch and router modules
Network management	Visualize and secure the WLAN. WCS for location tracking, RF management, wireless IPS, and WLC management
Mobility services	Applications such as wireless IP phones, location appliances, and RF firewalls

Cisco wireless IP phones have the same features as Cisco wired IP phones and can use LEAP for authentication.

The Cisco Compatible Extensions Program tests other vendors' devices for compatibility with Cisco wireless products. Using products certified by this program ensures full functionality of Cisco enhancements and proprietary extensions.

Characteristics of Wireless LANs

WLANs function similarly to Ethernet LANs with the access point providing connectivity to the rest of the network as would a switch. The physical layer is radio waves, rather than wires. IEEE 802.11standard defines the physical and data link specifications, including the use of MAC addresses. The same protocols (such as IP) and applications (such as IPsec) can run over both wired and wireless LANs.

The following lists some characteristics of wireless LANs and the data transmitted over wireless networks.

- WLANs use Carrier Sense Multi-Access/Collision Avoidance (CSMA/CA).

- Wireless data is half-duplex. CSMA/CA uses Request to Send (RTS) and Clear to Send (CTS) messages to avoid collisions.

- Radio waves have unique potential issues. They are susceptible to interference, multipath distortion, and noise. Their coverage area can be blocked by building features, such as elevators. The signal might reach outside the building and lead to privacy issues.

- WLAN hosts have no physical network connection. They are often mobile and often battery-powered. The wireless network design must accommodate this.

- WLANs must adhere to each country's RF standards.

Service Set Identifiers (SSID)

An SSID maps to a VLAN and can be used to segment users into groups requiring different security or QoS treatment. SSIDs can be broadcast by the access point or statically configured on the client, but the client must have the same SSID as the AP to register with it. SSID names are case sensitive. When multiple SSIDs/VLANs are used on an AP, the wired connection back to the network must be a trunk to carry all the VLANs.

WLAN Topologies

The use of wireless products falls into three categories:

- Client access, which allows mobile users to access the wired LAN resources

- Wireless connections between buildings

- Wireless mesh

Wireless connections can be made in *ad-hoc* mode or *infrastructure* mode. Ad-hoc mode (or Independent Basic Service Set [IBSS]) is simply a group of computers talking wirelessly to each other with no access point (AP). It is limited in range and functionality. Infrastructure mode's BSS uses one AP to connect clients. The range of the AP's signal, called its microcell, must encompass all clients. The Extended Service Set (ESS) uses multiple APs with overlapping microcells to cover all clients. Microcells should overlap by 10–15 percent for data and 15–20 percent for voice traffic. Each AP should use a different channel. "Pico" cells, with even smaller coverage areas, can also be used.

Workgroup bridges connect to devices without a wireless network interface card (NIC) to allow their access to the wireless network.

Wireless mesh networks can span large distances because only the edge APs connect to the wired network. The intermediate APs connect wirelessly to multiple other APs and act as repeaters for them. Each AP has multiple paths through the wireless network. The Adaptive Wireless Path (AWP) protocol runs between APs to determine the best path to the wired network. APs choose backup paths if the best path fails.

Client Connectivity

Clients associate with an access point as follows:

Access points send out beacons announcing information such as SSID, unless configured not to.

Step 1. The client sends a probe request and listens for beacons and probe responses.

Step 2. The AP sends a probe response.

Step 3. The client initiates an association to the AP. 802.1x authentication, and any other security information is sent to the AP.

Step 4. The AP accepts the association. SSID and MAC address information is exchanged.

Step 5. The AP adds the client's MAC address to its association table.

Clients can roam between APs, but the APs must be configured with the same SSIDs/VLANs and security settings. Layer 2 roaming is done between APs on the same subnet and managed by the switches using a multicast protocol: Inter-Access Point Protocol (IAPP). Layer 3 roaming is done between APs on different subnets and is managed by the wireless LAN controllers. The switch connected to the AP updates its MAC address table when a client roams.

Short roaming times are needed for VoIP to reduce delay. A client will attempt to roam (or associate with another AP) when

- It misses too many beacons from the AP.

- The data rate is reduced.

- The maximum data retry count is exceeded.

- It is configured to search for another AP at regular intervals.

Cisco Wireless Network Components

Cisco supports two types of wireless solutions: one using autonomous access points, and one using lightweight (or "dumb") access points in combination with WLAN controllers. The wired network infrastructure is the same for both types: switches and routers.

Access points can receive their power from Power over Ethernet (PoE) switches, routers with PoE switch modules, or midspan power injectors, thus alleviating the need for electrical outlets near them. APs require up to 15 W of power, so plan your power budget accordingly.

Autonomous (Stand-alone) APs

Autonomous APs run Cisco IOS, are programmed individually, and act independently. They can be centrally managed with the CiscoWorks Wireless LAN Solution Engine (WLSE), can use Cisco Secure Access Control Server (ACS) for RADIUS and TACAS+ authentication, and Wireless Domain Services (WDS) for RF management. Redundancy consists of multiple APs.

Network Design for Autonomous APs

When using stand-alone APs, the traffic flow is from client to AP to connected switch, and from there into the rest of the network. Plan the SSIDs and VLANs that will be on each AP, keeping in mind any roaming that users might do. Autonomous APs support Layer 2 roaming only, so SSIDs and VLAN must be statically configured on every AP in which a user might roam. Make sure to include a management VLAN on the AP.

Ensure that the AP has a power source, either a PoE switch or a power injector. Configure the switch interface connected to the AP as a trunk if the AP has multiple VLANs.

Lightweight Access Points

Lightweight APs divide the 802.11 processing between the AP and a Cisco Wireless LAN Controller (WLC). This is sometimes called "split MAC," because they split the functions of the MAC layer, Layer 2. Their management components also include the Wireless Control System (WCS) and a location-tracking appliance. Redundancy consists of multiple WLCs. The AP handles real-time processes, and the WLC handles processes such as:

- Authentication

- Client association/mobility management

- Security management

- QoS policies

- VLAN tagging

- Forwarding of user traffic

The Lightweight Access Point Protocol (LWAPP) supports the split MAC function in traffic between a lightweight AP and its controller. LWAPP uses AES-encrypted control messages and encapsulates, but does not encrypt, data traffic.

Controllers and APs can also use a new IETF-standard protocol to communicate with each other: the Control and Provisioning of Wireless Access Points (CAPWAP) protocol. CAPWAP operates very much like LWAPP.

Both LWAPP and CAPWAP operate over UDP. The controller does not have to be in the same broadcast domain and IP subnet, just IP reachable. Lightweight APs follows this process to discover their controller:

Step 1.   The AP requests a DHCP address. The DHCP response includes the management IP address of one or more WLCs.

Step 2.   The AP sends an LWAPP or CAPWAP Discovery Request message to each WLC.

Step 3.   The WLCs respond with an LWAPP or CAPWAP Discovery Response that includes the number of APs currently associated to it.

Step 4.   The AP sends a Join Request to the WLC with the fewest APs associated to it.

Step 5.   The WLC responds with a Join Response message; the AP and the controller mutually authenticate each other and derive encryption keys to be used with future control messages. The WLC then configures the AP with settings, such as SSIDs, channels, security settings, and 802.11 parameters.

Network Design for Lightweight APs

When using lightweight APs the traffic flow is from the AP, through the network, to the controller, and from there out to the rest of the network. User traffic is tunneled between the AP and the controller. Make sure that the AP and controller have Layer 3 connectivity.

The controller placement can be distributed, with a controller in each building or at each site, if no roaming between buildings is needed. A centralized design, with redundant controllers placed together, such as in a data center, simplifies management and increases user mobility.

SSIDs and VLANs must be planned, just as with an autonomous AP. But the configuration is done on the controller. Clients are placed into VLANs based either on the controller they connect to or an authentication process. The management VLAN is mapped to the controller. Controllers support both Layer 2 and Layer 3 roaming.

The link between a lightweight AP and the switch is an access port, assigned to a VLAN. The link between the controller and its connected switch is a trunk link. Controllers with several switch links can create an Etherchannel to the switch to increase bandwidth. Link aggregation is recommended for the 4400 series and is required on the WiSM and the 3750G integrated controllers.

Ensure that the AP has a power source, either a PoE switch or a power injector.

Wireless LAN Controllers

Cisco WLAN controllers can be either an appliance, a module, or integrated into a 3750G switch. In the appliance line, the 5500 series is meant for large deployments and, as of this writing, supports up to 250 APs. The 4400 series is for medium-sized deployments and supports from 12 APs to 100 APs. The 2100 series is for small deployments and supports from 6 APs to 25 APs.

The WLAN controller integrated into a Cisco 3750G switch can support up to 25 APs per switch, or 100 per switch stack. The Wireless Services Module (WiSM) can be installed into Cisco 6500 and 7600 series switches for large deployments that need support for up to 300 APs. Cisco ISR routers have a WLAN controller module that can support up to 25 APs for small deployments.

Hybrid Remote Edge Access Point (H-REAP)

Wireless controllers need not be in the same physical location as their associated APs. However, having an AP and its controller separated by a WAN link can lead to some inefficiencies and problems. Two clients in the remote location that need to connect would have their traffic tunneled over the WAN to the controller and back again. Additionally, the AP would lose functionality if the WAN were down.

H-REAP addresses these problems:

- **Connected mode:** When the controller is reachable, the AP transmits user authentication to the controller. It sends traffic in specified WLANs (usually local traffic) to its local switch, however, rather than tunneling it back to the controller. The connection from the AP to switch needs to be a trunk link if the AP handles multiple VLANs. Traffic bound to remote networks is still tunneled over the WAN to the controller.

- **Disconnected mode:** When the controller is not reachable, the AP authenticates clients itself. It still sends client to its connected switch, but of course remote locations will not be reachable if the WAN is down.

H-REAP is configured at the controller for any APs that operate in this mode.

Integrating Wireless into the LAN

This section covers configuring your switches for wireless APs and controllers, and planning your installation.

Switch Configuration

When the switch port connects to a stand-alone AP, configure it as an access port if the AP has only one VLAN and a trunk port if it has multiple VLANs. Trust CoS if the link is a trunk. Set the trunk native VLAN to the AP's management VLAN. Prioritize voice if you use wireless phones.

When the switch port connects to a controller-based AP, the port should be an access port. The port should be placed into the management VLAN because it is used for traffic between the AP and the controller. Trust DSCP on the port. If using wireless IPT, also set up QoS to prioritize voice.

The switch port connecting to a WLAN controller should be configured as a trunk link. Limit the trunk to wireless and management VLANs. Trust CoS and prioritize voice if you use wireless IP phones.

Links to a 4400 series controller might be aggregated into a Layer 2 Etherchannel. The 4400 cannot negotiate aggregation, so it is important to set the channel-group mode to "On". Otherwise, the configuration is the same as with any other Etherchannel. Configure the channel as a trunk, allow only the management and wireless VLANs, and trust CoS.

The WiSM requires a separate VLAN for its management. This VLAN should be assigned only to the module's service port and should not be used outside of the switch. Assign the VLAN to the service port with the global command **wism service-vlan** *vlan*. Assign an IP address to the VLAN interface; this IP address is used to communicate with the WiSM. The WiSM contains eight logical ports that connect to the switch fabric in two Etherchannel bundles. It also contains two separate controllers. Bundle configuration is done at each controller, using the **wism module** *slot#* **controller** *controller#* set of global commands.

Planning for a Wireless Implementation

In planning a wireless implementation, first gather requirements. Some questions to ask include the following:

- How many APs and where will they be installed?
- Stand-alone or controller-based?
- If controller-based, where will the controllers be located?
- Is PoE available?
- What VLANs and SSIDs will be used?
- What are the bandwidth requirements?

- What are the QoS requirements?

- Do you need security such as ACLs or Radius server?

- Do you need UPS for controllers?

When the requirements are gathered, create an implementation plan with details such as:

- Total needs, from the requirements that were previously gathered

- Any changes needed to the network design

- Any additional equipment needed

- Implementation steps

- Testing plan

The test plan might include checking that the AP and its clients get a DHCP address, that the AP is reachable from a management station, that clients can reach the network and Internet, and that the controller can reach the Radius server if used. To troubleshoot problems with wireless connectivity, review the steps for an AP to register with a WLC and a client with an AP.

NOTES

NOTES

NOTES

NOTES

NOTES

NOTES

NOTES

NOTES

NOTES

NOTES

NOTES

NOTES

NOTES

NOTES

NOTES

NOTES

NOTES

NOTES